Praise for *Sales Engagement*

"This book is packed with Next Gen strategies and tactics I was able to take back to my team and implement right away. Hearing not only from the Outreach team, but also their customers, was a terrific way of learning more about the value of Sales Engagement. As someone who trains hundreds of reps per year at a growth-oriented company, I highly recommend this book to sales reps, managers, and leaders looking to build the most efficient and effective sales processes."

—Jake Reni, Enterprise Sales Manager and Head of Adobe Sales Academy at Adobe Inc.

"There are a lot of things I could say positively about the future of Sales Engagement. Prospecting into enterprise companies can be challenging, specifically reaching the decision-maker. With our Sales Engagement Platform underpinning our strategy, we have found that our connection rates are incredibly high—we talk to the decision-makers on average 12% of the time, with an overall connection rate of 22%. We are referred 5% of the time by those decision-makers when emailed. The Outreach team knows Sales Engagement better than anyone else in sales today."

—Jennifer Brandenburg, Vice President of Worldwide Inside Sales at GE Digital

"Ask anyone about what matters to me: they would agree that I care immensely about personalizing our business interactions for richer client engagement. Outreach is the only scalable solution I've found that allows companies of any size to initiate meaningful discussions without sacrificing the personal, more human touch. Beyond this, our teams are able to easily measure the effectiveness of their campaigns. Outreach allows us to hone in on best practices and winning sequences that improve opportunity creation, pipeline building and ultimately, sales bookings. So who better to write the book on Sales Engagement than them!? I consider this a must read for any sales leader, period."

—Amy Slater, Vice President of Corporate Sales at Palo Alto Networks

"A problematic divide has developed in the world of modern buying and selling. On one hand, 80% of customers say the buying experience a company provides is as important as its products and services. In fact, the importance of personalization in the buying process has now eclipsed solution fit when it comes to winning your customer's business. On the other hand, sellers are busier than ever, spending only 1/3 of their time actually selling with the remainder spent on research, meetings, and administrative tasks. Having led large sales teams where personalization at scale and sales rep efficiency were so critical for converting prospects into customers, Sales Engagement platforms like Outreach need to be part of every modern sales team's technology stack. This book will give you the blueprint for success."

—David Priemer, Former VP of Sales at Salesforce and
Current Chief Sales Scientist at Cerebral Selling

"This book is a must-read for anyone who is trying to build a high-performance sales organization. Outreach has been walking the walk with their product for years and has finally put together *the* book detailing their most cutting edge strategies. There is no one better than Manny, Max, and Mark to write a book on Sales Engagement. Finally, we are able to allow our top reps to get 2X as much done per day, while our entry-level sales reps can learn from their team at lightning speed. Thank you, Outreach! Sales wouldn't be the same without you."

—Tito Bohrt, CEO of AltiSales

"Today's sales leaders overwhelmingly name Sales Engagement as their top priority. They are focused on the quality and volume of sales reps' engagement with buyers as they look to drive higher conversion rates and larger average deal sizes. Sales Engagement is such a high priority that 90% of sales leaders plan to invest in technologies and methodologies to help their sellers engage effectively with prospects and customers. As the leader, Outreach is well positioned to write the definitive book on sales engagement."

—Craig Rosenberg, Chief Analyst at TOPO Inc.

"On average, sales reps dedicate 15% of their time to manual activities like prospecting, which have a lower yield than other selling activities. Sales Engagement tools are emerging as a critical element for increasing prospecting efficiency and effectiveness."

—Steve Silver, Senior Research Director at SiriusDecisions

"In modern sales, sellers need to rethink the way they interact and communicate with buyers and ensure that they have the modern sales tools needed to create an engaging relationship. Sales Engagement is one of the hottest new categories on G2 Crowd and is becoming a must-have in every sales technology stack."

—Michael Fauscette, Chief Research Officer at G2 Crowd

SALES
ENGAGEMENT

HOW THE WORLD'S FASTEST-
GROWING COMPANIES ARE
MODERNIZING SALES THROUGH
HUMANIZATION AT SCALE

MANNY
MEDINA

MAX
ALTSCHULER

MARK
KOSOGLOW

WILEY

Contents

Preface

Sales Engagement: Why We Do What We Do

S ales is an art. Yet salespeople get a bad rap. This unfair discrepancy is the reason we started our company, Outreach.

I genuinely love salespeople. Hell, salespeople make the world go 'round.

Without salespeople, society as we know it would crumble. The word *salesy* is derogatory, yet the entire edifice of capitalism is built on the brunt of their hard work. Ideas, visions, and dreams have to be sold before they become real and start bringing in revenue. In fact, just about everything we enjoy or depend on (food, gadgets, films, sports, wine, health care, apps, music, art, travel, etc.) begins with a sale. Our economy quite literally depends on salespeople's ability to endure an entire day of rejection and still get up the next morning and do it all over again.

And there's plenty of rejection to go around. In sales, you are always on blast. Show me another profession where your performance is so cut and dried for everyone to see. You may think of professional sports or reality shows, but that's exactly my point. Those professions receive fame and glory (or at least infamy), whereas sales gets a negative rap. In sales, you get the ruthlessness without the chance of a red carpet. You either make the number and get to play another round—or you don't and are shown the door. It's the only job where the score gets cleared every quarter and you're only as good as your last deal.

When you think about it, sales should be the ultimate profession to draw inspiration from. After all, the best salespeople embody so many of the core values we hold dear in any other context: tenacity, determination, positivity, hope. Salespeople are required to go out on a limb. They must overcome their insecurities. They must roll with the punches, which come from all sides: their back-breaking schedules, their old-school leaders, and a harsh world that views them unkindly. These are all qualities people consider admirable in any other setting. Why is sales the cruel exception?

The Mantle of Despite

The plot thickens when we get into tools and technology. As it turns out, it's not just the court of public opinion that keeps salespeople down. The entire deck is stacked against salespeople. Theirs is the mantle of "despite." They sell *despite* pointless forecast calls that eat up their precious selling time. They sell *despite* arcane tools like Customer Relationship Managers (CRMs) that have them logging details instead of closing deals. They sell *despite* the noise, the distractions, and the pressure. We've all heard the stat that salespeople spend less than 36% of their time selling. Yet they're expected to hit blockbuster goals in this bare minimum amount of time.

When you define the problem this way, it becomes a moral imperative to help salespeople.

Moral imperative is a term coined by the philosopher Immanuel Kant,[1] and it often denotes the compelling need to fix something you cannot ethically tolerate. I love salespeople, and I just can't sit idly by while they struggle using outdated solutions and selling resources—knowing that my team has already built and tested the technologies to make a material difference. I simply cannot ethically tolerate a world where the very people who help make it work for the rest of humanity continue to endure needless pain without the tools that will make their unenviable jobs easier.

Hell, sales is tough enough as it is.

My Whirlwind Romance with Sales

I love salespeople because I've been a salesperson. I was the first Sales Development Rep (SDR) at Outreach when we were too broke to afford anyone with actual selling skills. Yet I managed to sell the company's first 60 customers personally. And I did it by hand. It was hard, often thankless, exhausting work. During those lean days, it was the love stories that kept me going.

My sales experience taught me a lot of things. First, euphoria doesn't come from closing deals. It's from learning from excited customers that your product phenomenally works and that it drives transformation not only in their numbers and workflows but also in their mindsets and cultures.

I tried selling to many segments and discovered that tech startups tend to adopt faster than most. I sold a few licenses to a technographics firm called Datanyze and worked with Jason Vargas, Managing Director of Outbound Sales.

When Jason shared how Outreach empowered his team to achieve a more than 50% reply rate, I became the most ecstatic SDR on the planet. So I visited Jason's team and discovered they were mostly

---

[1] Kant actually described a *categorical imperative*, a standard of rationality representing the supreme principle of morality. See, for example, https://plato.stanford.edu/entries/kant-moral/.

ambitious people in their 20s trying to do their best at their first corporate job. They felt great about the experience and appreciated the energy modern Sales Engagement technology and best practices infused into their sales process.

Within just two quarters of implementing Outreach, Jason's team doubled its revenue.

It was an awesome achievement for them. It was an aha moment for me. It was when the love I felt for salespeople became requited, instead of a one-way romance.

And it wasn't a fluke. The same success and transformation that happened at Datanyze got replicated elsewhere—at global tech enterprises such as Cloudera and AppDynamics and in local businesses such as the Green Lizard Towing Company in North Carolina.

The emergence of Sales Engagement is changing the calculus for businesses. But more importantly, it is leveling the playing field for motivated salespeople who are trying their best to achieve the impossible for their team, company, career, and customers.

At the end of the day, the world needs salespeople to keep businesses profitable and the economy healthy. But given the lousy cards they are dealt with at the onset, salespeople also need every piece of assistance they can get.

So, yes, I do it for the love of sales. It is my dream and great honor to create a transformative solution that, if I'm very lucky, salespeople will love in return. This is the modern era of Sales Engagement, and it is the future of sales.

Manny Medina

CEO and Founder of Outreach

It was a warm fall September day in San Francisco when I got the phone call that would change everything. I was notified that I got the business development job at an early stage company called Udemy. I would be in charge of building the sales side of the marketplace.

It was a euphoric feeling—I got the job! Soon after, though, reality hit. In this role, I would be expected to build a sales process at a company that had extremely high growth goals and extremely low resources. This meant we had to be unbelievably efficient with our sales process.

A challenge like this is sometimes exactly what you need. You look in the mirror and say, "OK. If I had to streamline the entire sales process, with no wasted motions and effort, what would it look like?"

I realized I needed to think differently. I needed a foolproof way to get prospects' attention. I needed to break through the noise. I needed a way to get in front of the buyer, wherever and however they consumed sales communications. I needed to be able to easily test everything from subject lines to calls to action to call scripts to voicemail intros. A way to scale my sales communications without sacrificing personalization. A way to easily follow up with potential buyers without having to write the email and physically press send each time. A way that leveraged multiple channels so we could meet the buyer where they wanted to meet, whether it was on LinkedIn, via email, over the phone, sending a gift, recording a personalized video, or meeting with them face-to-face at a conference. You guessed it: I needed to create a modern Sales Engagement strategy.

The Sales Engagement Era

I spent the past five years building a media company called Sales Hacker, which continues to provide educational content to more than 100,000 subscribers on all things sales. Our content contributors are practitioners and leaders at the fastest-growing companies in the world. The industry has evolved at a rapid pace and in an incredible way, and I've been lucky to have both a bird's-eye view and inside track. Sales Engagement is our most sought-after topic.

Through Outreach, I've spent the past six months talking to modern sellers and sales leaders, from some of the world's hottest startups to Fortune 500 stalwarts, about Sales Engagement. These are our prospects and customers who are currently leading the industry or looking to take it to the next level. It is undeniable across the board. A dramatic change in sales is upon us.

This is a new era—a time where there are more options for the buyer than ever before. More information at their fingertips. More companies doing similar things. More salespeople to contact them about it.

Salespeople need to be ready. They need a whole new education and suite of technology. I'm here to tell you that it has arrived.

It's time to be where the buyer is. It's time to be testing and optimizing your outreach. It's time to be relevant. It's time to be personal. It's time to embrace the modern era of Sales Engagement.

Companies doing this right are growing revenues at rates never seen before. Read on to learn the secrets to how they're leveraging modern Sales Engagement.

Max Altschuler

VP of Marketing, Outreach
and CEO, Sales Hacker

I was 16 years old, working my first job, standing in the middle of the entrance to the most horribly named shoe store in the world, The Athlete's Foot. My blue, logoed polo shirt and khaki pants were complemented with some real fresh kicks (yes, my sneaker game is still strong). "So many bad shoes," I thought as I looked at people's feet in the mall traffic sauntering by. That's when it hit me. A revelation. I could just keep standing there waiting for someone to walk in the store, or I could start engaging with people to get them to come into the store. My job wasn't just to sell shoes; it was to help people understand they *needed* me to sell them shoes.

You might ask why someone would need me to sell them shoes. Simple answer: because an early sales mentor of mine (thank you, Michelle McGee) taught me how to find the perfect shoe for the person I was serving. I wasn't selling shoes. I was selling a better morning run. Which meant I was selling a healthier heart and warding off the risk of obesity. Which meant I was selling more time to spend with kids and grandkids and the chance to watch them grow up. I wasn't selling shoes. I was selling the sharp kicks that would complete the interview outfit. The shoes that would give that final boost of confidence as they walked in the door to that potential new job. I was a great salesperson that knew my product, could diagnose a problem, and cared about the person in front of me.

There was only one hitch: Nobody knew how much I could help them. I was the friend they didn't know they had. I was a shoe guru hidden in a temple at the mountain's summit helping only the people willing to climb to the top and visit me.

I needed to change my actions based on these new motivations. Standing in the store and waiting for them to come see me was no longer acceptable, so I decided to stand *outside* the store to engage people.

Two obvious things happened almost immediately. First, I was rejected more. As a skinny, pimple-faced teenage nerd in the marching band, I had thick skin, so this didn't bother me. What did affect me, though, was the other thing that happened: My monthly bonus checks started getting much larger. Much, much larger.

I outsold everyone in my store. I outsold everyone in the seven-store franchise. In fewer than 20 hours per week, I outsold the full-time workers. Once I intentionally engaged with people—not to make a sale but to get them to understand how I could help them—I became a shoe-selling superhero.

As time went on and technology evolved, it became necessary to ask the next question: What is the digital equivalent of standing outside the store instead of inside it? How do you stand out in a person's inbox when it's so crowded that it makes the line at the Orange Julius in the late '90s look tiny?

That's when I met Manny Medina through a mutual friend. Manny just happened to be trying to figure out if he could sell this new technology to solve this exact challenge. I saw the demo, and I was amazed by what I saw. It's what I always wanted but didn't know was possible. That's when I learned that the digital equivalent I sought had a name: Sales Engagement.

I immediately made the move to buy Outreach's Sales Engagement Platform for my team. A couple weeks later, as I was doing some trainings for my previous job in the Seattle area, I reached out to Manny to see if he wanted to meet up. He introduced me to Andrew Kinzer, Co-founder of Outreach, and we had coffee underneath the famous Lenin statue in Fremont. Manny and I talked shortly after and geeked out on sales and sales technology. Throughout our ongoing conversations, I became so inspired that I approached Manny about selling Outreach. His response? "We can't afford you." I offered to sell on a 100% commission compensation plan and still remember his exact words in response to that offer. Manny said, "We can afford that! Let's go. I'll send you leads tonight."

Sure enough, I got the leads that night, quit my job two days later (with the full blessing of my wife and four kids), and started a five-month trek to selling $1 MM worth of Outreach. I was joined by four other people willing to follow me, one of whom flourished and is still one of our best sales reps, Theron Glenny.

Fast-forward three years, and I still have never regretted this decision. In fact, I love Sales Engagement and Outreach so much that we host 20 Outreachers at our Thanksgiving table every year—now that's love.

My goal for this book is to share my inspiration with you and show you what's so great about Sales Engagement so that you can begin your own transformative journey. I did, and I truly hope you will too.

Mark Kosoglow

Vice President of Sales at
Outreach

Lastly, we didn't want this book to be about us three, and it's certainly not a book about a software company. It's a book about a movement. An unfair advantage emerging in sales today that will definitely be here for the foreseeable future. That movement is Sales Engagement, and it's being created by an entire community of forward-thinking sales leaders.

In order to do it justice, we made sure to provide varying perspectives from leaders of that community. These are our savviest Sales Engagement-focused thought leaders, customers, partners, practitioners, and executives from a vast array of companies and industries.

This book isn't a silver bullet. Nothing in sales is. But it can be your guidebook, your idea sparker, your framework foundation, and much more.

We know it's a game changer, and we hope you feel it too.

Who This Book Is for

There is only one prerequisite for readers of this book: It's for anyone interested in leveling up their game and anyone who is inspired by the idea of doing more than they ever thought possible.

For nine out of 10 people, audacious goals are the stuff of overwhelm. This book is for the odd one out—the one in 10 who goes against the flow. The rare soul. The moon landers. The four-minute milers. The person who is inspired—not intimidated—by the idea of breaking records. If you'd rather take action and make moves, then this book is for you. If you find yourself questioning whether long-held limits are absolute or just arbitrary, come along as we take you on a journey on a rocket ship. These pages will ignite your imagination on how to test those very limits and perhaps raise the standards of human achievement in your field.

This book is not meant for people already satisfied with the comforts and familiarity of the way things are. Instead, this book unmasks the most poignant challenges of tomorrow and explores the rich opportunities for individuals and teams who dare to look at mastering the future. This book is for anyone who wants to play full out, wherever they are. It is for the young Sales Development Rep, prospector, or cold caller/e-mailer who dreams of hitting their number for the first time.

It's for the Account Executive still struggling to hit their number consistently. It's for the Senior Account Executive who's mastered the basics and now wants to break a personal record. It's for the sales leader who dreams of creating a world-class org that will be revered as a shining industry example—the stuff of keynote speeches and case studies. It is for the Sales Operations Specialist who, behind the scenes, is quietly and methodically architecting an epic workflow that will quadruple productivity but who will probably never get a thank you, let alone get invited to President's Club. It is for the Customer Success Manager who inherits the efforts of all the above and puts on a smile and fulfills the hell out of those grand sales promises, even if it means answering the phone on a holiday or advising on yet another strategy after an endless day of work.

Only people who actively want to make a difference and transcend the inertia of the daily grind can hope to appreciate and apply the nuggets of tactical wisdom that line the chapters of this book. Only professionals who ask the right questions and seek new, better, and smarter solutions to their business problems can hope to glean anything of value from this pioneering work.

This book is for anyone fascinated by the idea of greatness and what it takes to truly achieve it.

If you share this passion or fit this description, then this book is definitely for you. Within its pages are insights, tactical tips, and practical solutions that will address your most urgent pain points and finally move the needle on your personal or team performance.

Although this book focuses on results and sales performance, anyone who wants to shake things up and change things for the better can benefit from reading it:

- Sales Managers who have tried everything Sales Ops and Sales Enablement recommended but whose teams still generate subpar outcomes
- Startup Founders who have reached the critical point at which their companies need to scale at a ridiculous rate just to achieve

their board's new set of targets or meet the expectations of a new but demanding VC, who just joined the party

- Enterprise VPs of Sales or Chief Revenue Officers (CROs) looking to future-proof their organizations by adopting cutting-edge technologies, frameworks, and best practices
- Sales Ops and Sales Enablement leaders looking to build modern sales organizations that provide the company an unfair advantage
- Customer Success teams who want to enhance their offers and generate more value from each customer lifecycle through improved Sales and Customer Engagement
- Ambitious part-cycle or full-cycle sales reps who want to achieve crazy levels of success in the easiest and most efficient way possible

This book targets people who don't merely want to win; they want to redefine what it means to win. Sure, they want to make their number—but they also want to make history. They want to leave a legacy. When people ask, "Who's the best _____ (insert sales function here) you know?" These knowledgeable responders will always say your name.

This book is for the ones who want to play big and win big and bask in the glory when they do. This book is for you.

SALES
ENGAGEMENT

1

Sales Engagement: Why It's So Important

Chapter 1

The State of Modern Sales

The modern Sales organization is under unbelievable pressure. Quotas are higher than ever. Resources are the leanest they've ever been. So of course the modern Sales org is a well-oiled machine, running on all cylinders to create the maximum output possible, right?

Wrong.

In fact, the level of efficiency in the modern Sales org is startlingly bleak. According to the CMO Council, lost productivity and poorly managed leads cost companies at least $1 trillion every year.[1] Yes, that's trillion with a *t*.

What accounts for this chasm? How can there be such low efficiency when expectations are so high? Surely Sales leaders are motivated to create the highest-functioning orgs possible, considering it is their necks on the line? Indeed, they are. But Sales leaders are not to blame.

Instead, an unholy trifecta hobbles even the most motivated, high-achieving Sales org into a no-win situation. Together with changing consumer behavior, business practices, and sales technologies,

---

[1] https://www.cmocouncil.org/thought-leadership/programs/lead-flow-that-helps-you-grow

these factors help define the modern sales floor. They portray a chaotic landscape replete with shifting priorities, changing roles, formidable challenges, and emerging imperatives. However, this new reality offers scant clues on how Sales organizations should navigate the new terrain and come out undisputed as winners. If you are a sales professional today, you simply aren't set up for success.

Common Factors Holding Your Sales Org Back

1. Overwhelming administrative work
2. Lack of sufficient data for driving desired sales outcomes
3. Outdated frameworks, mindsets, and technology solutions

Let's look at them in more detail.

1. Overwhelming Administrative Work

Ask a sales rep or an Account Executive what takes much of their time at work, and chances are they'll enumerate a litany of tedious administrative tasks. Updating customer records and other CRM data, tedious forecast meetings, jumping from one sales software to another, reading and composing e-mails, looking up contact information, and enduring long, torturous moments of analysis paralysis are just some of the activities that sap the souls of modern sellers and consume the largest chunk of their working/waking hours.

In fact, the need to perform noncore/nonselling tasks compels already overwhelmed sales reps to spend only a third of their time actually selling, according to an alarming study by Salesforce. And that, of course, leads to the more alarming statistic of falling quota attainment rates:

According to a study done by Salesforce, nearly 60% of sales reps expect to miss their 2018 quotas pretty much because they don't have enough time to sell.

2. Lack of Data

Big data and business intelligence have been industry-moving buzz-words for some time, but the efficiency and impact of these resources in the field of sales have just started to mature—especially when it comes to low-funnel reporting such as revenue attribution, opportunity attribution, and tying dollars to activities.

Truth be told, sales has been lamentably unscientific for decades. The good news is that emerging technologies now offer exciting new data breakthroughs. Unfortunately, not every Sales org has gotten the memo.

Lead prioritization, revenue forecasting, context-based engagement, and visibility in customer intent are just some of the areas where sufficient data need to be collected and optimized. Without the right data in the right amount, customer engagement will remain intuition-driven, which simply is not enough anymore to improve metrics. Certainly human intuition, sales experience, and street wisdom will remain relevant, but the heavy lifting will be performed by data-crunching algorithms. Without these data-driven systems, Sales organizations stand to lose valuable opportunities to convert leads and nurture customers.

3. Outdated Technology Solutions

As always, technology plays the role of a key enabler in the world of sales. From the Rolodex to CRM, from rudimentary telephone systems to advanced Voice Over Internet Protocol (VOIP) and video conferencing networks, technology helps transition a Sales organization to a new business reality.

The trouble is technologies almost always evolve much faster than the organizations that use them.

The vast majority of Sales organizations, for example, make do with outdated technologies until (i) their more agile and forward-looking competitors have adopted game-changing solutions; (ii) their sales performance has become so untenable that they are forced to seek technologies that can move the needle; or (iii) they lose enough top producers that they sit up and pay attention. By then, these Sales organizations often realize they have a lot of ground to cover just to catch up with smarter competitors—or that more powerful solutions than the one they finally adopted are already being launched in the market. They are officially behind the curve.

Today, having a decent CRM platform is a mere baseline, not an end-all, be-all resource. Artificial intelligence and machine learning rule the current conversation, along with one-to-one video, chatbots, and SMS texting, to name a few. Sales organizations need to embrace the brave new world and take full advantage of the array of solutions available to them. Yet most orgs still rely on anachronistic technology, with which smart reps succeed despite, not because of.

So How Do You Crack the Success Code?

If you're a Sales leader, how do you get reps focused on meaningful, revenue-generating activities? If you're a rep, how do you do more in less time? How does the whole Sales org work together to hit the number without encountering burnout and morale issues?

If you're in sales, how do you stop choosing between hitting your number and seeing your kids' baseball games or ballet recitals? How do you do both?

Believe it or not, there is a solution that solves all these problems.

Sales Engagement: The Next Step in the Communication Revolution

The answer is Sales Engagement. Following in the footsteps of e-mail and smartphones, Sales Engagement is the next communication revolution.

Once upon a time, the telephone revolutionized the way we communicate. Then, mobile phones made landlines obsolete. After that, e-mail came along and kicked snail mail out. Now is the era of Sales Engagement.

In the same way we laugh at the rotary phone now, salespeople will also look back on the time before Sales Engagement was a thing—and laugh at how ridiculously inefficient manual sales communication was. In manual sales communication, practitioners lack the software automations that help them perform their jobs faster and better.

Now, sales professionals access rich data-driven insight for prioritizing leads and designing sales activities, discern the best communication approach for each specific customer, and optimize value and revenue for their organizations.

By combining the best capabilities of human sellers and artificial intelligence, Sales Engagement brings system and science to the art of selling, making it easier and faster for businesses to reach customers at the right moment, on the right channel and to engage them with the right message. *It makes it possible to humanize sales at scale.*

Driven by artificial intelligence and data analytics, Sales Engagement tools enable salespeople to automate tedious tasks and allocate more time for personally interacting with customers and performing other valuable sales activities that require a human touch.

As Mark Kosoglow, Vice President of Sales at Outreach, puts it, "The ability to stand out in the crowd and help people understand why they need your help is something that must become part of your sales DNA. Even if you care, your technique is flawless, and your product impactful, if no one knows who you are or why you can help, you will always be fighting an uphill battle for sales success. This is why Sales Engagement is so important. It helps reps break through the noise to even get to share how fantastic their product is in the first place."

And that's just the tip of the iceberg. Many people think of Sales Engagement as a seller's (or marketer's) ability to get someone to notice them. That is definitely a big part of effective Sales Engagement, but there is much more to it.

Great salespeople are constantly engaging their prospects. Let me give you some examples. A deal that has gone dark needs to be engaged. The new decision maker introduced in a late-stage sales meeting needs to be engaged. The technical buyer who can't say yes, but definitely can say no, needs to be engaged. Your internal resources (e.g., sales engineers, subject matter experts [SMEs], etc.) need to be engaged.

Engagement is defined as to attract, occupy, or employ; to establish a meaningful connection with; and to bring weapons together in preparation of fighting (wait a sec, you'll get why I put this one here …).

Modern Sales Engagement means sellers must not only get buyers' attention (traditional understanding), but they must also occupy that attention and use it to establish meaningful connections. Then, once connections have been made, they get a chance to use those sales techniques, product knowledge, and positioning like a weapon to save a company from itself.

I once learned that companies are nothing more than large political organizations designed to prevent money from being spent; hence, sellers must rescue companies from their own inertia and desire to maintain the status quo. For a great seller, nothing is better than the touching of the gloves to begin the fight. And though that metaphor implies winners and losers, it isn't meant to because great sellers always create a situation where everyone wins.

How Difficult Is It to Adopt a Sales Engagement Mindset?

Sales Engagement is already making significant inroads for early adopters. The good news is that barriers to adoption are basically nonexistent. The most powerful Sales Engagement solutions are sophisticated products at the bit-level, but they are insanely simple and easy to integrate and use with any existing sales technology stack or sales process, much like a plug-and-play device.

All you need are Sales leaders looking to take their team to the next level and motivated reps who want to make a difference for their career, their organization, and their customers.

Chapter 2

How Sales Engagement Solves Seven Major Business Pain Points

The days of old-school communications have passed. In their stead, we have new modern sales communications that are data-driven, personalized, relevant, omnichannel, sequenced, and fully optimized for today's sophisticated buyer.

Fear of missing out (FOMO) is not for closers. It's for those who don't take advantage of modern Sales Engagement best practices.

Sales Engagement enriches the buyer journey, however complex it might become. At the same time, it also enables sellers to do more than they ever thought possible: You can hit quota with ease, achieve predictable revenue in your org, and even attend your kid's ballet recital without missing your number. Sound too good to be true?

Not so fast. Don't be the person who called e-mail a fad. Don't be Burt Reynolds when he passed on the James Bond role (true story). Don't be HBO when they passed on *Mad Men*. Instead, stay with us and learn how Sales Engagement squarely solves your seven major business pain points.

11

Seven Major Business Pain Points Solved by Sales Engagement

1. Not optimizing for how the modern buyer likes to buy (generational, always-on, omnichannel, etc.)
2. Lack of Revenue Efficiency (doing more with less) with a growth-focused team
3. The manual nature of sales and why reps have so little time to sell
4. Lack of consistent, repeatable, data-driven processes
5. Improving new hire time to value
6. Lack of data to drive business decisions
7. Tech stack troubles (why CRM, phone, and e-mail are no longer enough)

Business Pain Point #1: Not Optimizing for the Modern Buyer

Selling to buyers the way they like to be sold to is not a novel concept, yet with all the channels in existence today, it's not as simple as it sounds. From new forms of communication (hello, texting) to generation gaps between baby boomers and millennials (and welcome, gen Z), there are more selling factors than ever before.

Then there are factors like the role of the person you're trying to reach. For example, a sales professional or executive might respond better to mobile-based messaging because they live on their phones and are never at their computers. This might be a text or short LinkedIn message. At the same time, an operations or IT professional might work out of two screens and prefer only screen-based communications like longer e-mails or value-driven content like e-books or whitepapers.

Throw in the fact that traditional channels are more saturated than ever before, and you have a recipe for poor performance if you're not optimizing your sales process for the modern buyer.

Business Pain Point #2: Lack of Revenue Efficiency

As we alluded to at the beginning of the book, Sales organizations are under unprecedented pressure. Quotas are the highest they've ever been. Resources are at their leanest. So how can you achieve success within a modern Sales org? By achieving peak Revenue Efficiency—that is, getting the maximum return for the minimal amount of resources invested.

> *"Revenue Efficiency is the true north of every Sales leader."*
>
> —*Manny Medina, CEO of Outreach*

Revenue Efficiency isn't an abstract term; it's a practical (and achievable) goal for every Sales and Marketing leader. But with so many variables and levers, how and where do you start to ensure your team maximizes results with the minimum resource expenditure?

Revenue Efficiency encompasses the following:

- How to evaluate your org structure to support better Sales and Marketing alignment
- How to leverage joint attribution to create an efficient, collaborative environment
- How to bypass vanity metrics in favor of low-funnel, revenue-oriented analysis
- Finding the right bridge technology to boost efficiency and streamline workflows

Sales Engagement is a powerful ally in the quest for Revenue Efficiency. Sales Engagement offers traditional metrics like volume of sales activities, but it doesn't stop there. Sales Engagement offers true revenue attribution, meaning it shows not just sales activity but also *whether that activity resulted in revenue*. This killer differentiator means predictable revenue goes from a pipe dream to a pipeline reality.

Business Pain Point #3: The Manual Nature of Sales and Why Reps Have So Little Time to Sell

We've all read the statistic, from CSO Insights, about how sellers spend only 36% of their time selling. Burdensome administrative tasks and sales technology that can be described only as user–unfriendly are some of the main culprits behind this lack of meaningful activity.

Sales Engagement empowers a rep to do more activity in less time, thanks to capabilities like automated e-mail follow-up (a transformative time-saver within itself) and automated meeting reschedules. Sales Engagement means if it doesn't require specialized strategic work, a rep is not wasting valuable time on it. This new category of technology also empowers reps to work smarter, not harder, with blueprints for success like winning e-mail templates and sales scripts so there's no need to reinvent the wheel.

As an added benefit, a good Sales Engagement Platform (SEP) is actually created with the end user in mind, which should make for an even better buying experience for your next potential customer.

Business Pain Point #4: Lack of Consistent, Repeatable Data-driven Processes

Most sales leaders want to build a reliable machine. They want to know with reasonable certainty that if they put X amount of raw materials in one side of the machine, Y will come out the other side.

In a modern sales environment, the only way to do that is to create consistent, repeatable processes and playbooks. There's a defined set of playbooks that are used consistently for handling inbound leads, doing outbound prospecting, closing new business, and managing relationships with current customers.

Business Pain Point #5: Improving New Hire Time to Value

Improving new sales rep ramp time, even by a small fraction, can be a major game changer. In an enterprise Sales org, new rep ramp times are typically months. It can be even half a year or longer! Imagine if all your reps could hit quotas even just one month earlier. That would be *significant* boost in revenue for your business. This is just another area where optimization comes into play.

In order to optimize new rep ramp, you need a repeatable, scalable data-driven process that can be easily replicated. Get your whole team hitting quota, and hitting it sooner, without any extra admin or effort from their managers and execs. That's the goal, and that's what's possible.

Business Pain Point #6: Lack of Data to Drive Business Decisions

In the modern era of sales, gut is just not good enough anymore. Your competitors are using machine-learning, natural language-programming, powered data to make informed decisions. So when the board or the boss asks about this quarter's numbers, don't be the one leaving it to chance.

Data and tech have arrived. There are no excuses anymore, but there are things that have your back. Data that tell a story without bias. People can talk the talk, but numbers walk the walk, and they'll save your job one day. Never make an informed, strictly gut decision in your sales process again.

Business Pain Point #7: Tech Stack Troubles

Why dial number by number when you can use software that'll save you time? Why e-mail from your inbox when there's software that can track and measure response rates, set up multivariable tests for subject lines and copy, and allow you to share best practices across the team? Why not be centralized? Why not allow reps to automate menial tasks that take away from selling time? The money you spend on sales software will be returned to you in spades when productivity, efficiency, and effectiveness are through the roof. It's one of the few functions in a company where this is so insanely important.

We are in the dawn of a new day. The sales tech stack has arrived. CRM, phone, and e-mail are no longer enough. The days of the Sales Engagement Platform are here. Don't get stuck in the dark ages.

In Part 2 of this book, we'll dive into actionable, tactical, and practical ways Sales Engagement can solve all of these major business pain points and more.

PART

2

Diving Deeper: Essential Elements of a Strong Sales Engagement Strategy

Chapter 3

Humanizing Sales with Personas, Personalization, and Relevance

At Outreach, we work with thousands of high-growth-focused sales organizations. We get the privilege of picking the brains of some of the most forward-thinking and successful sales leaders every week.

The most frequent challenge we hear from these leaders is balancing e-mail quantity and e-mail quality.

We're here to tell you that personalization at scale is a challenge, but it can be done.

Mark's Take: The Three Main Types of E-mail Customization and the Pros and Cons of Each

Let's start with reviewing the three types of e-mail customization. E-mail customization must be solved for on three distinct levels: account, persona, and hyper-personalized. At Outreach, we initially solved for account-based customization. This was a deliberate decision, so let me explain so you don't have to screw up like we did. Then we'll cover persona-based customization and hyper-personalization.

1. **Account-based customization**: Account-based customization involves looking at the specific challenges and goals of a company, versus those of a role.

    Pros:

    - You create content that can be used across an entire account, regardless of role.
    - It makes your communication very tailored for a specific account.
    - It can help reps have better conversations as there will be a high level of intelligence specific to the company.
    - It allows you to go faster as reps use "talking points" across multiple contacts in an account.

    Cons:

    - If you aren't on target with messaging, your efforts will fall flat.
    - It's not hyper-personalized on the individual (which is advised for your very best prospects).
    - It can be time-consuming and requires the ability to make sense of lots of information.
    - Sometimes, company goals don't align with the personal goals of the prospects you are reaching out to.

2. **Persona-based customization**: This is customization for role-based challenges. Personas are buckets of people with like responsibilities (and possibly titles) across different companies. For example, Account Managers typically have the same set of functions, responsibilities, and challenges no matter who they work for what or the business model is.

    Pros:

    - It can be applied across roles at multiple accounts, which allows you to prospect much faster.

- Challenge sets are more intimate to the individual you are reaching out to, as opposed to company challenges. ("Account Managers are the unsung heroes of the org" versus "congratulations on going public!")
- It gives reps the ability to be much more empathetic in their messaging.
- Content can be applied to large sets of prospects/communications.

Cons:

- Role value statements are more difficult to construct in a meaningful way.
- Not all titles are universal, so sometimes messaging misses the mark.
- If your company sells to many roles, there can be a lot of content to create.

3. **Hyper-personalization**: This is customization at the person (not persona) level—that is, personalization aimed at the individual.

To hyper-personalize e-mails, you need to research a specific person, their likes/dislikes, challenges, tendencies, beliefs, hobbies, responsibilities, etc. E-mails of this type are handcrafted for the individual to which they are written.

Pros:

- It can be highly effective.
- You display a level of care and thoughtfulness that resonates with prospects.
- It helps reps to really understand the people they are reaching out to.
- Knowledge gained can be leveraged throughout the sales cycle.

Cons:

- It is extremely time-consuming.
- It is difficult to scale without serious resources.
- It requires a level of expertise and experience to do well and to do well consistently.
- It can be hard to find appropriate data to do correctly.

Hyper-personalization Wins Every Time, Right? Wrong.

Many people think, "We're just going to write a bunch of hyper-personalized e-mails, and everybody is going to get back to us because of all the time and effort we showed making sure our value proposition resonated with each person as an individual." But this may not always be the most effective way. How do you know which way to go?

Ultimately, data showed us what worked best for us. If you don't have visibility into the effectiveness of your messaging, this is an impossible choice to make. The stakes are too high to get it wrong. Complicating the choice further is this: At different stages and in different seasons of your company's life, one approach will work better than another. The best approach is in flux—OK not only for the company but also for the accounts and people you are reaching out to. We are all addicted to sales because it's fast-paced and ever-changing; unfortunately, so are our accounts and prospects. People move into new roles, needs change, politics shift, etc. It's very hard to stay on top of all the variables.

"You can look at a 10-K, an annual report, or the transcript of a quarterly earnings call to find great information for public companies to customize communications. A company's LinkedIn page, blog, Twitter feed, or marketing materials (white papers, case studies, e-books) can give you ideas for private companies."

—Mark Kosoglow, Vice President of Sales at Outreach

The Number One Technique I Do Not Recommend Is Choosing More Than One Technique

Whatever you decide, I warn against tackling multiple strategies at once. The amount of content you are required to create will be voluminous and can slow down your efforts—or derail them entirely. To illustrate, if you are targeting seven account-level challenges and four personas, you would need to produce 28 separate pieces of content to support your messaging. If you have reps doing hyper-personalization at the same time, then all the work on account and persona messaging won't be used as much. Instead, carve out your most important prospects to receive the "hyper-personalization love." For everyone else, stick to account-based or persona-based.

Account Sourcing: How We Do It at Outreach

At Outreach, we have interns source accounts under the guidance of our Director of Sales Operations. Those account lists are enriched, scrubbed, tiered, assigned, and loaded into Salesforce on behalf of our reps. We do not allow reps to create accounts in our CRM.

The Benefits of Reps Not Creating Accounts Directly in Our CRM

- Eliminates duplicate account issues
- Prevents expensive reps from wasting time on manual work
- Avoids "territory" disputes
- Ensures reps are not wasting time prospecting accounts
- Normalizes account distribution (i.e., makes sure everyone has the same number of OK, good, and great accounts)
- Eliminates discrepancies and creates a squeaky-clean instance of Salesforce

How does Sales Ops source accounts? There is a litany of data providers that can help with this (ZoomInfo, DiscoverOrg, InsideView, DataFox, etc.), but let me share a couple of tactics that might help you get creative.

Both tactics begin with creating an Ideal Customer Profile (ICP) that has five to seven parameters (geography, technology adopted, size, industry, Alexa rank, offerings, etc.). Tactic 1 is as simple as entering those parameters into a software solution that spits out the companies that meet that search criteria. Choosing one provider will standardize your data. Export it into your CRM. Tactic 2 involves using offshore resources (like those found on upwork.com) to source accounts that meet those criteria into a spreadsheet you can load into your CRM.

Either way, you'll need to lock the ability to edit accounts by anyone other than an operations employee. Create a process (we use a ticketing system inside Salesforce.com) that allows reps to request data changes. This ensures that data stays consistent and reps don't spend time sourcing accounts or changing verified data points.

Now that you have the accounts your team needs to work, make sure you are set up to research them and apply that research to the contacts.

Clear and easy-to-understand rules around how reps should fill an account with contacts is essential. Your sales reps wield a powerful weapon when prospecting. Not providing them a framework to follow means you are increasing your chances of unproductive, ineffectual prospecting.

The accounts and prospects your reps put into the machine might be one of the most important business decisions your organization makes on a daily basis. You can't afford to leave this to chance.

Here is the seven-step process we use at Outreach:

- Develop a title search query for LinkedIn[1] that returns only prospects most productive to engage.
- Put it in a doc, etc. where a rep can copy it.
- Have reps paste the search string in LinkedIn to find contacts at accounts in your territory.
- Click into each result.
- Use ZoomInfo ReachOut product to get e-mail and direct dial information.
- Export contacts into each account.
- Rinse and repeat until you have plenty of prospects.

---

[1] https://blog.linkedin.com/2007/07/15/5-tips-on-how-t

By pasting a prepared Boolean search string into the title field of LinkedIn, our reps are lightning-fast at finding only the prospects our Sales Operations team has deemed attractive without having to learn advanced techniques. This saves endless scrolling looking for people a rep might deem interesting (and rabbit trails going off in all directions because they see something that catches their eye that has nothing to do with sales results).

Having tons of great contacts to target is great, but it is dangerous to target every contact at once. Many mail servers begin to flag sellers as spam if they think reps from your domain are hitting them with too many e-mails. We have a rule of engagement for an account and its contacts to avoid this from happening: It's called Rule 5-2.

It tells reps to target five contacts in an account at a time, with at least two of them being management level or greater. We continuously add new contacts into our messaging as others are removed (for positive or negative reasons) so reps are always in compliance with the rule. Our SEP also sends data to Salesforce that allows us to create reports, giving our reps instant, up-to-the-minute visibility into accounts needing additional contacts engaged.

Without a clear set of rules that defines what "working an account" actually means, reps will create their own internal rules. I love being able to use "group think" to create best-of-breed solutions with tons of buy-in from the team. However, a huge range of approaches is good for testing but typically doesn't allow for efficiency and adaptability. In my experience, most reps want to do what is most effective, regardless of whose idea it is.

Surfacing these rules is a priority for a sales leader when striking the e-mail quality/quantity balance.

Crafting a quality e-mail message doesn't have to be difficult or time-consuming. When we capture research about an account at Outreach, we classify it into a "research bucket." A bucket, or category, groups companies based on their current situation or status to see which triggers are getting the best results so we can tailor messaging to those buckets. More important, our list of buckets keeps reps focused on and hyperaware of what bits of useful information to look for and how to deal with them once uncovered.

An example of a bucket is recruiting vibrancies: If our research shows that a company is doing a lot of hiring in the Sales department, this might indicate the account is dealing with aggressive sales goals and would benefit from a solution like Outreach. Other examples of buckets or categories might be good quarter results, bad quarter results, new product launching, new leadership hire, certain technologies being used, certain LinkedIn profile characteristics, and so on.

E-mail quality requires research, as table stakes. The challenge is how to leverage research across multiple e-mails/accounts/scenarios. How can the research done for one person be used for another in that account? How can the solutions used to solve the challenge of what a rep's research uncovers be used in the next account's messaging too? Buckets are our answer to those questions.

Additionally, knowing what is on the "sales scavenger hunt list" helps a rep look for only those things. If you have to find a car with a Vermont license plate, you begin to quickly assess and identify license plate locations, colors, placements, etc. You become fast and good at scanning cars for plates in general and assessing if they meet the criteria of your list. Same thing for buckets. Having a list of buckets helps guide your reps' research so that they become experts at knowing where and how to identify a company that has a problem they know can be solved. It builds confidence in finding accounts, as well as pitching them.

We use a spreadsheet detailing each bucket/category and all the points of customization that can be used while crafting custom e-mails to accounts in that group. We also use buckets for phone call "scripts." Each bucket includes four or five open-ended questions a rep can ask to start an e-mail or a phone call, two or three value propositions a rep can make relating to the bucket, one or two case studies applicable to the bucket that a rep can attach to or cite in the e-mail, or a related customer quotation that reps use to allow our customers to sell on our behalf.

This provides a lot of structure. Do your research, bucket it, and then, when you're writing your e-mail, go to the corresponding bucket and decide which bits and pieces you want to use to customize it. Structure is the friend of productivity.

You're probably wondering where the buckets and corresponding documents come from. They are developed by the whole sales team. When a new bucket is identified, based on the research our team is doing, it is updated in the bucket spreadsheet. The reps create all aspects of the document and request the needed case study(ies) from the Marketing Department. Reps are the people closest the customer, and their group knowledge around what prospects want is invaluable.

Existing bucket document components are fine-tuned during the monthly meetings, also based on what's working and what's not. The actual performance results of e-mail components are shown in reports generated by Outreach.

A clear process, combined with the right infrastructure and tools, ensures a balance of quality and quantity e-mails by your sales team.

How does a sales rep balance e-mail quality with e-mail quantity? It's incumbent upon the sales leader to create a well-thought-out process that leverages workflow, research, and sales automation. The Outreach sales team tackles this problem to execute, on average, 1,000 personalized e-mails per rep per week. I want to emphasize that our solution was built upon dozens of rep-to-rep conversations, failed ideas, rep input, meetings, and a total team effort to tackle this problem.

We'll go deeper into sequences and omnichannel outreach in the next chapter.

But first, let's continue.

Why Seller-Focused Content Is Destined to Lose

If your business still runs on seller-focused templates or scripts, then it is doomed to fail. Only brands that deliver a modern buying experience will have a foothold in a customer-centric universe.

It is up to the sellers to do their homework and to immediately ditch lazy, wide-net, vanilla approaches that tend to only discourage key segment(s) of their buyer market from fully engaging their brand. Instead, businesses need to deliver a modern buying experience by customizing engagement strategies for both medium and message.

So how do you get that all-important communication sequence right?

Empathy.

Sell by Embracing an Empathy Mindset

This sounds trite, but embracing an empathy mindset is the right place to start. When you are creating a sequence or planning your talk track, you need to think—*really* think—about the buyer. And to view things from their vantage point. What is an average day in their life like? What do they want? What annoys them? By practicing empathy, the overwhelming process of planning a winning sequence becomes simple.

For example, if you are thinking about how to sell to a Sales Operations Administrator, start by picturing what a day in their job is like. The work of a Sales Ops professional is extremely complex, detail-oriented, and technical. So as you plan your sequence, do you really think interrupting them with a jarring phone call is the way to go?

Of course not. Sales Ops professionals tend to be very regimented, meticulous people. They most likely have designated times when they check their e-mail. Therefore, a perfect Sales Ops sequence begins with a noninterruptive approach like an e-mail they can check when they have time. Another approach might be a creative direct mail piece, including noise-canceling headphones, a funny Do Not Disturb Sign, or a plant for their desk to brighten their workspace.

What about when you're trying to prospect a VP of Sales? VPs are the polar opposite of heads-down Sales Ops pros. VPs of Sales certainly have their heads-down time when they are preparing a big client pitch or crunching numbers for the next forecast. But by and large, VPs of Sales are on the move. If it's a Field VP, they spend a significant amount of time in their car, commuting or going on prospect meetings. So be creative: Make them a brief podcast with your sales pitch that they can listen to as they drive.

VPs of Sales also favor short, snappy soundbite messaging, so a quick text or a one-to-one personalized video might work well.

Are your wheels turning yet? By embracing an empathy mindset, you can engage the modern buyer more quickly and more powerfully.

Psychology Meets Technology

You don't have to do all this manually. Sales Engagement is the Sherlock Holmes to your Sigmund Freud, serving up sales intelligence that gives you handy clues into the interior life of your buyer persona: What time of day is the prospect most responsive? Did their company just go public? How's the weather where they live?

> "'Congrats on the recent funding announcement!' beats out 'I saw from our mutual LinkedIn connection' any day."
>
> —Mark Kosoglow, Vice President of Sales at Outreach

When you start from a place of empathy, you can build more powerful and more meaningful connections. Sales Engagement adopts the empathy mindset and uses technology to make it easy, doable, and scalable. Being in sales is hard enough. So take advantage of smart shortcuts to quickly deliver the most meaningful experience possible.

Stuck on how to reach out? If you use an SEP, the data should show you whether a phone call, an e-mail, or some other form of communication would work best with your buyer.

Stumped on how to message them? Sales Engagement data provides easy icebreakers, such as the following:

- Their last LinkedIn post
- Their competitors
- Recent company news and press releases
- Twitter posts
- Company details (industry, size, etc.)
- Account and prospect notes
- Historical activity and engagement
- The local weather in the prospect's town
- The local time
- Whether their company just merged or got acquired

Modern Sales Engagement offers the buyer intelligence to create the perfect buying experience, right down to the time of day that the buyer is most responsive.

To help us provide another point of view, we brought in Sales Development expert and long-time Outreach friend and customer, Jason Vargas, Co-founder of CopyShoppe.co.[2] Jason brings more than 15 years of experience in the Sales Development leadership role to the table, so when he speaks, we listen.

Jason has three pillars to an efficient and powerful Sales Engagement strategy:

- Personalization: "Is this thoughtful and genuine?"
- Automation: "Can I maintain this type of quality and productivity while being completely hands-off?"
- Optimization: "Am I making an intelligent decision supported by data?"

According to Jason, these practices are often misunderstood and can easily be applied incorrectly. Here is his simple framework that will change your whole approach. Let's have him break it down.

---

[2] https://www.copyshoppe.co/

Jason's Take: The Biggest Myth About Automation

When thinking about automation, let's start by first defining its root word, *automatic*: done or occurring spontaneously, without conscious thought or intention.[3] This definition can be further broken down to execution without planning. Ironically, the goal of automation in the sense of sales automation is actually the opposite. A solid Sales Engagement strategy that includes automation must include an immense amount of planning in order to cut through the noise of the mediocre canned e-mails that drown your inbox.

Yes, I know you may be thinking, "I am automating to save time. If it is so much work, why would I bother?" Although a strong automation strategy requires significant upfront planning, once you have the formula nailed, it works seamlessly and can be scaled to save you tons of time in the long run. As the distinguished Dwight D. Eisenhower once said, "In preparing for battle, I have always found that plans are useless but planning is indispensable."

Personalize

Research your buyers. In order to understand your buyers, you must first understand their preferences and motives. So, to better understand your prospects, ask yourself a few questions during your research:

- Who and where are my buyers?
- What communication channels do my prospects prefer?
- How do these organizations buy software?
  - Do these organizations have a formal buying committee? (Demandbase says 59% of companies do.[4])
- Does their industry tonality skew toward formal or informal?
- What is their motivation to buy my product?

---

[3] Oxford Dictionaries: https://en.oxforddictionaries.com/definition/us/automatic
[4] http://e61c88871f1fbaa6388d-c1e3bb10b0333d7ff7aa972d61f8c669.r29.cf1.rackcdn.com/DGR_DG061_SURV_B2BBuyers_Jun_2017_Final.pdf

Write compelling e-mail copy. E-mail copy must be personalized; strong, personable writing is not something you can automate or outsource to a robot. E-mail copy is often the most overlooked component in sales. Although it may seem unimportant, copy is absolutely something that you need to invest in. This is one of the biggest no-brainers to outsource to an expert or hire as a specific role. If your copy is underperforming, use self-awareness, put your ego to the side, and allocate money in the budget for a professional copywriting firm or headcount.

Three Reasons to Invest in Personalized E-mail Copy

- You don't have the time (a study found that sales reps spend less than 36% of their time selling).[5]
- At scale, minuscule increases in reply rates and conversions translate into massive increases in pipeline dollars (a marginal increase of 1% to your reply rate over approximately 6 months [250 e-mails per week] is 62 additional conversations).
- Writing is not your sales rep's forte—inexperienced writers tend to write from a product or brand perspective, rather than from the buyer's perspective.

An Academy Award Approach to Copywriting

If you do decide to undertake e-mail copywriting yourself, or as an action for your sales reps to do, try to transform your e-mail copy from the standard, self-motivated, feature-laden messaging to the old adage why-me-why-now approach. The easiest way to personalize is to write an e-mail sequence like an Oscar-winning film. That is, an e-mail sequence with a thoughtful, *value-driven* storyline (sequence strategy) focused on the buyer's needs—not your solution. I practice this by writing sales e-mails without mentioning the name of my product at all, and I challenge you to do the same. Remember to use multiple acts (e-mails) that build off

---

[5] https://www.forbes.com/sites/kenkrogue/2018/01/10/why-sales-reps-spend-less-than-36-of-time-selling-and-less-than-18-in-crm/1

each other, slowly unveiling why your prospect should be working with you right now and ultimately ending in the climax (call to action).

Consider your favorite award-winning movie. Whether you're into gangster films like *The Godfather* or classic feel-goods like *Forrest Gump*, they have some things in common. You get to know a hero, a villain, or main character as the plot unfolds. Life lessons are often revealed in unexpected scenes. They build tension through foreshadowing, strong character development, and flashbacks.

So how can you accomplish this level of mastery in your cold e-mail copy? The key is building momentum and not giving everything away too soon.

Set your scene: What background do you have on your buyers? How can you mirror flashbacks by speaking to life before your product/service versus after?

Bring the unexpected: How can you deliver value to your buyers without just throwing sales and marketing collateral their way? How creative can you get, and how can you teach your buyers something relevant to their challenges and your value prop?

Develop connections: Just like viewers get to know main characters, build the relationship with your buyers before you ask them for their time. Why should they trust you? What value have you brought them, and how can they relate personally to you and your brand?

Personalization Do's and Don'ts

Personalization is one of the most misinterpreted things in sales slang. Salespeople are often seen defining personalization as an effort to make a common connection with their prospect. They've got it all wrong. You need to personalize yourself and demonstrate humility. Your approach should not be flattery but instead genuinely you. Yes, booking the demo is important, but humble engagement is something that will generate far more than just a conversation. Here are real examples of how to engage and how not to engage.

Do: Mention a relevant, recent piece of thought leadership.

Example: "Hi, Jason. I really enjoyed your podcast on preventing a toxic work environment. My manager made it required listening for our entire team. I'd love to ask some questions that I had written down while listening."

This approach will work 90% of the time. The SDR clearly did their homework here and approached me like a real person, not a dollar sign. I hit the reply button before I even read the sales pitch.

Don't: Reference a lazy, generic fact.

Example: "Howdy, Jason. I see that you used to work at PunchTab. Did you enjoy your time there?"

This is generally what comes to mind when people describe personalization. But really, this is just a demonstration of laziness to me. Did the SDR choose PunchTab in an attempt to prove he scrolled farther down into my LinkedIn profile than his peers? I don't know the answer. The message could have been much improved if they had some sort of relationship to PunchTab, such as, "I see you used to work at PunchTab. My colleague interviewed there before joining XYZ company. Perhaps you interviewed her?"

The bottom line: Don't force personalization where it isn't relevant—just be yourself, and your prospects will respect that more than anything.

Automate, When to Send, and Why It Pays to Work Weekends

Design your send schedule. Once you've completed the elements of a Sales Engagement strategy that require a human touch, it's time to automate the ones that don't. There are a ton of articles out there about the best time to send sales e-mails. However, the definition of a successful send schedule is unique to every industry. For example, I'm a big fan of e-mailing on the weekends. A lot of people I talk to think this is pervasive and unprofessional, but let's face it—sales is pervasive by nature. If the majority of people are not sending e-mails at those times, why wouldn't you use this to your advantage?

The other piece to consider here is what you're measuring: If you don't know what you're measuring, how do you know if you've succeeded? Automation is multifaceted, so pick one or two key performance indicators (KPIs) to measure at a time.

Five Automation Metrics to Consider

- Click-through rates to drive people to a landing page
- Open rates to test deliverability or subject lines
- Reply rates that generate conversations
- Social shares to measure buzz
- Refer/forward to a friend to measure value

No matter how you crunch the numbers and what you're measuring, exceptional results come from testing and optimizing everything you can.

Continuous Improvement

A/B test and optimize your e-mails. An e-mail sequence is not static. Your buyers are constantly evolving, and so should your sales e-mails. If your goal is to improve e-mail performance, you must run tests, analyze the results, and make data-driven decisions based on the outcomes.

At CopyShoppe, we do this by using Outreach's Amplify feature. Through tons of A/B testing across our customer base, we've learned that one-word subject lines are effective in driving higher open rates. Due to this finding, we start campaigns off with several subject line tests, including a one-word variation.

Campaign results can sometimes be surprising and shed light on things you perhaps didn't consider during the initial launch. For one of my clients, their entire buyer persona changed based on the data. After analyzing the numbers, we tested a sample of title variations outside of their target buyer. Can you guess the results? Yep, we soon realized another department within their target accounts produced more buyer interest and ultimately more pipeline.

That's why it's important to allow the data to speak for itself and make strategic adjustments accordingly. And remember, when one A/B test ends, the next one starts.

Five E-mail Variables for A/B Testing

- Subject lines
- Send schedules/time of day (weekday business hours, weekday morning versus evening, weekends, etc.)
- Value proposition order (which e-mails and value propositions drive the most engagement)
- Tonality (formal versus informal, etc.)
- Testimonials and case studies (analyze if certain testimonials perform better than others within the same message)

Once you've successfully tested these variables, it's time to put that data to work! Take the winner of the A/B test and duplicate it. Leave one untouched and add another variable to the duplicate. Rinse and repeat. You should be optimizing each of your e-mail sequences at least once per month.

By knowing when to apply the human element, when to let technology do the job for you, and how to use data to weave it all together, you will achieve peak Revenue Efficiency in your org.[6]

---

[6] http://e61c88871f1fbaa6388d-c1e3bb10b0333d7ff7aa972d61f8c669.r29. cf1.rackcdn.com/DGR_DG061_SURV_B2BBuyers_Jun_2017_Final.pdf; https://healthypsych.com/psychology-tools-what-are-cognitive-distortions/; http://www.onlinepsychologydegree.net/2013/02/04/15-common-cognitive-distortions-that-may-be-behind-your-productivity-problems/

Jason did a fantastic job of summing that up for us, but humanization at scale doesn't stop there.

As mentioned previously, buyer personas are a great tool to help salespeople understand their customers better. Unfortunately, most teams struggle with creating personas that are actionable.

According to a 2016 report by Cintell, one of the top challenges that companies face with buyer personas is getting the organization to use them.

Why does this happen? Three reasons:

1. Most persona building projects don't engage the broader team involved in the delivery of the customer's desired outcome. This non-inclusive approach leads to personas that miss the other influencers in the buying decision.
2. The conventional models don't focus on identifying how the persona will be interacting with the product. Instead, they focus on representing broad goals, general motivations, and pain points, and they consider that to be a sufficiently clear picture.
3. Current approaches don't feature a clear vision of what success looks like for the persona. Everyone who interacts with your product doesn't have the same desired outcome. Every person/role involved in the buying process has a different definition of what success is. Your sales team needs to be able to understand the set of objectives for each role in easy-to-convey terms.

Now think about this: If your Sales Engagement goal is to accelerate your ability to personalize at scale, what happens if you attempt to accelerate that process without really understanding who your buyer is? You may accelerate that sale right into the closed/lost deal stage. Because this topic straddles sales and marketing so much, we brought one of the top subject matter experts on personas—Jen Spencer, VP of Sales and Marketing at SmartBug Media—to continue peeling back the layers of this onion.

Buyer insights from persona research can include the following:

- Learning what type of content is most likely to generate a response
- Learning how your future customer prefers to engage in the sales process
- Learning what specific problems your future customer needs to solve so your sales team can address those problems head-on

Beware of Demographic-based Personas

It's easy to fall into the pattern of documenting buyer personas based on role and market segment.

Here's an example of a commonly misused persona description:

Director of HR for a software company located in North America that has between 100 and 5,000 employees.

Although this information helps define the ICP, it provides no information about the individual. Let's call this person Hannah and add some additional market research to the mix:

Hannah is the Director of HR for a software company located in North America that has between 100 and 5,000 employees. Hannah is female, between the ages 35 of 55, and lives in the suburbs with her spouse and two young children.

We're getting closer with the additional demographic information, but what's missing from this buyer persona description is psychographic data: information about Hannah's attitude, interests, personality, values, opinions, and lifestyle.

Here's what a more effective buyer persona description might look like for Hannah:

Hannah is the Director of HR for a software company located in North America that has between 100 and 5,000 employees. Hannah is continually looking for solutions to keep employees connected and happy because she is partially measured on employee turnover. Hannah is female, between the ages of 35 and 55, and lives in the suburbs with her spouse and two young children. She's outgoing and personable—the type of person who lights up a room. Hannah goes to the Internet to seek solutions for every type of problem she encounters, but she also highly trusts referrals from her peers and professional organizations when it comes to making business decisions. Social media is her go-to resource for news and current trends. Due to her very busy schedule, Hannah tends to use her smartphone more than her laptop and getting her on a call during business hours is nearly impossible. You're likely to hear from Hannah via e-mail after 8 pm when she's catching up on the day. The later it is, the more emojis you can expect in her communications.

With the addition of some psychographic data, a sales rep now has a deeper understanding of what Hannah cares most about—and how to best communicate with her. Imagine if you didn't know these details about Hannah and you kept leaving voice mail messages at her office or you sent her large files to read that didn't display well on a mobile device.

Creating well-researched buyer personas that are based on live interviews with your actual customers is the first step toward being able to better serve future customers throughout their buying journey.

Implementing Persona Research in the Sales Process

A good salesperson knows that initial discovery can make or break a sale. Effective discovery provides a sales rep with critical details that will help that rep not only meet the buyer where he or she is on their journey but also more accurately qualify and forecast the opportunity.

With buyer persona research at their fingertips, sales reps now have a general idea of what's going to be most relevant to a person before having a live conversation. Although it's important to note that buyer persona research does not and should never replace sales discovery, this research enables a sales rep to go into a discovery call with a basic idea of the buyer's pains, how he or she measures success, and what he or she values.

In addition to these qualities, persona research also enables sales teams to tailor their communication efforts based on an individual's preferences.

Jen's Take: Appending Psychology with Technology

Buyer persona research is the first part of the puzzle. It provides a strong foundation, and live customer interviews provide invaluable color and texture on personality, habits, and work style that no algorithm could ever serve up. The beauty of adding a technology layer to a buyer persona is that it allows you to take the hypotheses you formed in your buyer research and confirm them with data. For example, in the case of Hannah, you have already hypothesized that because she is a busy mom, she will be most responsive after 8 pm when her kids are in bed and text will be the best way to reach her. This is an astute set of assumptions and certainly stands to reason. But why assume when you can confirm?

SEPs include features like best time of day to call, what communication channels have been most effective, and more. You don't have to guess which sales communication methods will best engage the buyer; you can know.

The cherry on the sundae? Once you crack the code for a perfect persona-based message, SEPs can send these messages at unprecedented speed and scale and then return data-driven insights. Thanks, Jen!

When it comes to sending messages, it really starts to get into the personalization and relevance of your content.

Here's how our customer Amy Slater, Vice President of Corporate Sales at Palo Alto Networks, is thinking about personalization at scale.

Amy said, "With 25 years of technology and sales leadership under my belt, it breaks my heart that many smart, sophisticated salespeople still think personalization looks like this:

Amy,

I have sent you multiple e-mails and voice mails to discuss our product XYZ with you and have not heard back from you. It is likely due to one of three reasons:

1. *You don't have time.*
2. *You are not interested.*
3. *You are a robot.*

"We need to remember that personalization is about creating a one-to-one human connection with the customer," Amy said. "Inserting a first name variable or writing an obviously canned e-mail like the one above doesn't cut it. You need to personalize in a way that is going to make the prospect or customer feel like you intimately understand their problems and think, 'Is this person reading my thoughts?' Obviously, there are also business realities at play, so how can companies achieve similar personalization and customer intimacy at scale without sacrificing the human element?"

1. Define success benchmarks so you know when you have hit the right balance of scale and personalization.
2. Know when to automate at scale.
   a. Early-stage companies need to establish clear guidance on data hygiene and customer contact management.
   b. Differentiate between market segments related to customer size and industry. One size doesn't fit all.
3. Ensure tight collaboration between sales and marketing to understand buyer personas and to avoid "marketing speak."
   a. To maintain the human element at scale, create a hybrid sales/marketing role to assist in campaign scripting and management.
   b. Hold regular meetings with sales and marketing to review metrics for success.

"When you consistently put yourself in the shoes of your prospects, you will maximize the benefits of automation and personalization at scale without sacrificing true human connection."

Most salespeople consider e-mail to be a primary communication channel. It remains a staple of Sales Engagement practices. Yet salespeople still struggle with e-mail and the craft of writing altogether.

Advertising icon David Ogilvy told his employees, "The better you write, the higher you go." Legendary blogger Leo Babauta said, "No matter how you use e-mail, no one you're e-mailing wants to read a long essay or respond to 10 questions. We are all busy, and we all value our time." Best-selling author Jeff Goins put it this way: "When attention is sparse, the people with the fewest, most important words win."

We're not going to get too deep into outbound e-mail copy in this book, as there are plenty of resources out there for copywriting and it's just too big of a topic to cover. It almost needs its own book. However, our good friend Ralph Barsi, Senior Director of Global Sales Development at ServiceNow, sent us some good quick advice we thought we'd share.

Ralph notes that salespeople who e-mail using these techniques quickly build momentum. These professionals earn replies and win business. They provide clarity and direction. They enrich their relationships and networks. They make it easy for people to work with them. Ralph's advice? When writing B2B cold e-mails, make sure to:

- Write short sentences. Each word must earn its right in the e-mail.
- Say what you need to say in five sentences or less.
- Include at least one question mark to evoke a response. Otherwise, your e-mail is simply information for the reader.
- The subject line should tell the reader what the e-mail is about.
- Postscripts are powerful when properly used.
- USING ALL CAPS MAKES READERS THINK YOU'RE YELLING AT THEM.
- Using only lowercase and shorthand cuz u like 2 makes readers think you're 12.

- Before sending, read e-mails aloud to gauge how conversational they are and how much they represent your voice, tone, and intent.
- Most people read e-mails on their mobile phones. If they scroll at all, you risk losing their attention (and response). Mind the aesthetics of your e-mails.
- Use yes–no questions sparingly. Ask open-ended questions.
- Use proper grammar. Not "we should of" but "we should have." Not "your going to like it" but "you're going to like it." Not "one for Deb and I" but "one for Deb and me."
- Instead of asking for a 15- or 30-minute call, ask if it's easier to talk on Wednesday morning or Thursday afternoon ... for just 5 minutes.
- Smile when you write. It will come through.

E-mail will remain at the core of Sales Engagement for generations. Take care of it, and it will take care of you.

We're with Ralph on this!

However, we talked at length about sales being personal, but it's not just about that; it's about being relevant too. Maybe even more so. Here's what I mean.

Max's Take: Relevance Is Key

One time I went to New York City to speak at a conference. When I got to the hotel, I realized I forgot a belt. Luckily, I was staying in Times Square. When I walked out of my hotel, sure enough, there was a man with a cart full of belts and wallets. I was in a mad rush to not be late to my speaking engagement, so I bought a belt. From a man with a cart. In Times Square.

I never thought this is something I would do, but it was *highly* relevant. Now, had I not needed a belt when I walked out of my hotel but the belt salesman had known what city I was from, would I still have bought the belt? Definitely not. I wouldn't have the need. That's the difference between personalization and relevance. It's more important to be relevant than it is to be personal, but it's still super important to be personal.

Relevance in sales is about solving a problem that they have, know they have, and have now. It can be big or small, but they have to have it for it to be relevant. There are many ways to figure out what's relevant to a buyer.

For public companies, you can use what's called a Form 10-K and go to their K1.

Use this link and plug in the company name of the public company you're researching: https://www.sec.gov/edgar/searchedgar/company-search.html.

Then click on the form in the left column titled 10-K. Under the table of contents, you'll see a link that says Risk Factors. You can use the information here to appeal to the company's risks and pain points to make your message relevant to the recipient.

Figure 3.1 shows what an example Risk Factors section looks like.

In this example, they detail that integrating acquired companies is hard to do and may affect their ability to hit their number for the next quarter. If I were selling customer success technology in this space, this would be an incredibly relevant thing to bring up in an ideal outreach sequence:

ITEM 1A.   RISK FACTORS

The risks and uncertainties described below are not the only ones facing us. Other events that we do not currently anticipate or that we currently deem immaterial also may affect our results of operations, cash flows and financial condition.

Risks Related to Our Business and Industry

If our security measures or those of our third-party data center hosting facilities, cloud computing platform providers, or third-party service partners, are breached, and unauthorized access is obtained to a customer's data, our data or our IT systems, or authorized access is blocked or disabled, our services may be perceived as not being secure, customers may curtail or stop using our services, and we may incur significant legal and financial exposure and liabilities.

Our services involve the storage and transmission of our customers' and our customers' customers' proprietary and other sensitive data, including financial information and other personally identifiable information. While we have security measures in place, they may be breached as a result of efforts by individuals or groups of hackers and sophisticated organizations, including state-sponsored organizations or nation-states. Our security measures could also be compromised by employee error or malfeasance, which could result in someone obtaining unauthorized access to, or denying authorized access to our IT systems, our customers' data or our data, including our intellectual property and other confidential business information. Additionally, third parties may attempt to fraudulently induce employees or customers into disclosing sensitive information such as user names, passwords or other information to gain access to our customers' data, our data or our IT systems.

Figure 3.1 An Example of the Risk Factors Section

I understand that you are having issues integrating new technologies, thus affecting the happiness of your current customers. What if we could provide you with an alert as to when a customer is unhappy so you can proactively fix the relationship? Would that be interesting to you?

Is much better than:

Hey {{first name}},
I see you work at {{company name}}. We have customer success software that helps protect against churn.
Are you in the market for a solution like this?

The first one shows you've done your research and tailored the message to their pain point. The second one is a blanket statement, and though more personalized, doesn't drill into their exact pain point.

This also helps you select which accounts to prioritize. You should always be prioritizing companies that need you the most, whether that's most urgently or that you will provide the biggest impact for.

Other ways to get relevant information to use in your outreach include:

- Through backchannels, like asking joint customers of yours and the company you're prospecting to
- Public data sources like Crunchbase and Owler
- News sites that are tech- or industry-specific (Maybe you see that Uber is having an issue with safety in a *New York Times* article. If your solution is relevant to that pain point and the decision maker, you can use that.)

I once mentored a women's entrepreneurship group, and one of the entrepreneurs was starting a company around teaching proper manners, behavior, and etiquette in the workplace. She wanted to know how to start selling in a scalable manner.

What should her pitch be? Whom should she contact? How should she contact them?

My advice was simple:

1. Go to a news site that recently exposed an issue about misconduct in the workplace.
2. Take a screenshot of the news story and headline.
3. Reach out to venture capital and private equity firms that invest in startups.
4. Include the screenshot in the top of the e-mail with the subject line: Don't Let This Happen to a Portfolio Company.
5. Then under the screenshot, write, "I can help. Let's talk."

She took my advice and it worked *consistently*! Why? A few reasons.

The overall message conveyed a fear. People mostly buy for one of two reasons: They buy for love, or they buy for fear. This one definitely moved the fear needle.

But the biggest reason why this worked is because it was extremely relevant to their current situation. If you were to ask these investors what kept them up at night, it would be a company doing something that would make them fail instantly. Something so bad that it would tarnish the brand of the investor. Just being associated with that company would be bad for them (especially now more than ever, when the general public is on high alert to this).

The simple image of this behavior being punished on the cover of a major news publication is enough to get the meeting. It's hyper-relevant and easy to digest.

Ben Salzman and Kyle Williams run Dogpatch Advisors, a firm specializing in Outbound Operations for some of the hottest tech companies. Ben and Kyle recommend that when you're adding images to e-mails, make sure to not overproduce them: "If it looks like something a designer spent 10 hours on, you break the whole narrative. People are suspicious of things that look too produced. The bar should be either a 'time-strapped designer' level or an 'enterprising account executive who had 30 minutes in PowerPoint' level. That's the quality you're looking for."

This is similar to my advice, which is to use a simple screenshot to say it matter of factly.

These tips, tactics, and strategies work for all channels of communication, whether it be an e-mail, phone call, voice mail, one-on-one personalized video, direct mail letter, gift, social media mention or message, or something else. Sales Engagement platforms tie them together. In our next chapter, we'll go deeper into how to use these channels in your outreach to maximize your impact and be present where the buyer wants you to be.

Chapter 4

The Future Is Omnichannel and That Future Is Now

Buyer behavior is ever-changing. Naturally, sales reps need to follow suit.

As new sales channels are being introduced, old sales channels become saturated. These waves come in cycles. One day, phone works; the next day, pundits will say that "cold calling is dead" and that e-mail is on fire, only to cycle out of favor a few short years later.

David Priemer, CEO of Cerebral Selling and former VP of Sales at Salesforce, summed it up well when he said, "Buyer behaviors and their resistance to sales tactics are evolving faster than ever before. Rather than taking a defensive stance, organizations that embrace and prepare for this new normal and can pivot seamlessly will have an unbeatable competitive advantage.

"In a selling environment that changes by the day, there are two key ingredients to cultivating high-impact sales tactics:

1. Never fall in love! Complacency breeds mediocrity. Keep learning and iterating to find the new winning formula, not just a new template. Often, it's an entirely new sequence and set of channels.

2. When you find a winning tactic that works, ensure every member of your team is able to execute it with conviction and consistency.

"You need to be embracing change, and then you need to know how to change at scale. The future of Sales Engagement is set up to help modern sales teams propagate winning, high-impact approaches, quickly and consistently," David says.

The buyer persona is changing as well. More and more decision makers and stakeholders are millennial or gen Z. Of course, this is only going to continue to compound. These folks are native to things like FaceTime video, texting, the iPhone, social media networks, photo sharing apps, and many other new methods of communication. This makes understanding how to evolve with the new trends affecting buyers even more important. The generational differences are getting more extreme as technology advances faster and faster.

There are many other factors at play here too—global factors such as General Data Protection Regulation (GDPR), which may make channels like e-mail less effective in certain countries. This means you'll have to find other channels to leverage in the sales process. However, one channel is never enough.

The answer is Omnichannel, the act of using multiple channels to sell to an individual or group of individuals.

Sales Hacker, the leading educational resource for B2B salespeople, recently surveyed 884 B2B buyers from startups generating annual sales of less than $20 million to robust enterprises reeling in north of $1 billion.[1] They uncovered that the patterns of modern buying behavior truly are changing with age, job function, technology, and many other factors. Therefore, understanding these factors will go a long way in helping B2B organizations discern which medium to use for specific buyer personas and which to optimize for specific engagement contexts, no matter whom you sell to.

---

[1] https://www.saleshacker.com/ultimate-sales-engagement-ebook

Here are some fascinating facts discovered by the study:

- LinkedIn consistently ranks very high on preferred contact medium, as well as on preferred channels for content consumption (see Figure 4.1).

About 70% agreed that they would respond to LinkedIn requests or InMail from sales reps. Of these responses, sales titles and executives were most likely to respond, whereas Operations professionals were least likely.

Out of all channels, LinkedIn was the winner (see Figure 4.2).

Some other interesting data points from the survey about modern sales channels include:

- More than half (53%) of respondents react positively to calls via the mobile numbers displayed in their e-mail signatures.
- E-mail remains the desired communication method for most roles, with 40% of executives and 51% of Operations professionals preferring the medium.
- It's important to meet your buyers where they are. Sales titles and executives answered positively to questions regarding their mobile devices. They can be called on their cellphones and left voice mails, and they are OK being texted. This is because they live on their mobile devices. On the flip side, Operations titles didn't like being contacted on their mobile devices. Their day-to-day workflow may require them to live on a computer monitor or two, so they prefer methods that allow them to be sold to where they want to be.

Make sure you are optimizing channels based on all factors. This is something to play with and A/B test, which you can learn more about in Chapter 5.

Modern sales is about understanding not just how people like to buy but also what mediums they use to make purchasing decisions. For example, when buying a new car, you can ask friends, go to online car purchasing forums to ask questions or read comments, go to sites like Consumer Reports that have reviews from notable sources, visit sites

I occasionally accept customized connection requests from sales reps.

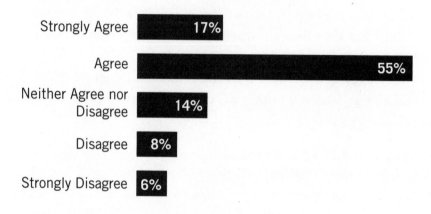

I occasionally respond to LinkedIn InMail from sales reps.

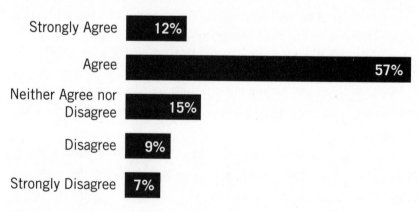

Figure 4.1 LinkedIn Content Consumption

What media is most likely to elicit your reply?

Figure 4.2 Media Most Likely to Elicit Replies

like Yelp to read peer-written reviews, watch commercials, or even talk to a sales rep. The same is true for software and many other products or services.

Peer-review sites like G2 Crowd, TrustRadius, and Capterra; forums and groups like MSP or the Sales Hacker community on LinkedIn Groups; local American Association of Inside Sales Professionals (AA-ISP) events; advertisements; webinars; whitepapers; e-books; and speaking to sales reps are all ways to make buying decisions now. There is more information for the buyer than ever before.

In a survey, Sales Hacker asked respondents about these mediums. As you can see in Figure 4.3, the answers at the top were fairly even, but when they dug deeper, the results got a little more interesting.

What media are you most likely to consume to solve business problems?

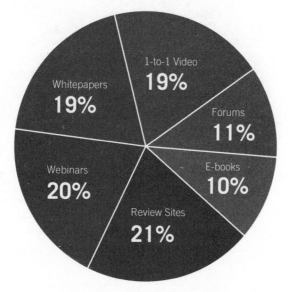

Figure 4.3 Media Most Likely to Solve Business Problems

The age of the buyer greatly influenced how they liked to receive information, as millennials and gen Z like to learn, act, and purchase differently than their predecessors (see Figures 4.4 and 4.5).

A study by CSO Insights backed this up.[2] They surveyed 500 B2B decision makers on how they liked to receive information when looking into a purchase. The highest-ranked factors were subject matter experts and review sites. By the way, hearing from a sales rep was all the way down at number nine on the list. With the way LinkedIn's newsfeed is set up today, anyone can be a subject matter expert—even you! It's never too late to start.

---

[2] https://www.csoinsights.com/wp-content/uploads/sites/5/2018/06/Growing-Buyer-Seller-Gap-White-paper_FINAL.pdf

Preferred media for ages 35 and older

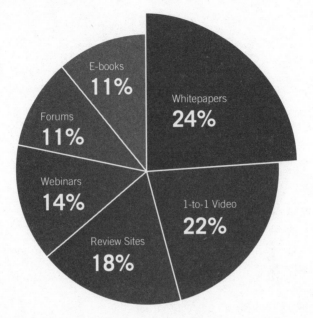

Figure 4.4 Preferred Media for Ages 35 and Older

It all goes to show you can't just customize the channel and the message for the modern buyer; you have to customize the medium also.

The entire buyer engagement survey can be found at salesengagement.com/buyer.

Sequences: The New Secret Weapon

The major channel types we'll go over in this book and highly recommend are:

- Phone
- Voice mail
- SMS/text

Preferred media for ages 35 and younger

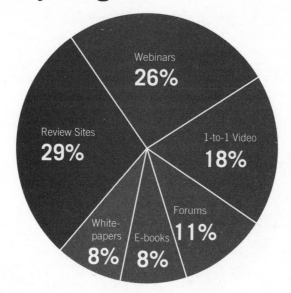

Figure 4.5 Preferred Media for Ages 35 and Younger

- E-mail
- LinkedIn
- One-to-one personalized video
- Direct mail and/or gifts
- Other social
- Events

Now that you have your channels, it's time to put it all together. The fact is one channel is no longer e-mail. You can send nine e-mails in 21 days, but you are way less likely to make meaningful contact unless you're coupling it with other channels, preferably in a tightly organized sequence.

What is a sequence? A sequence is a series of sales touchpoints separated by time used to achieve an outcome (for example, book a discovery call, get a cold deal heated back up, involve more decision makers, etc.) Those touchpoints occur across multiple channels (e-mail, phone, social, text, etc.) in automated or manual ways.

How Outreach Does Sequences

To improve productivity, set up a sequence of touchpoints your sales team needs to use for every lead/prospect. An SEP is required to inject automation into your process. Without some level of automation, you will not be able to significantly increase your quantity. We'll talk about how you can make mild increases by "building muscle" but not the step changes of productivity most sales teams desire. Depending on the goal, a sequence might look something like this:

Day 1: Customized e-mail written by rep

Day 1: Phone call with voice mail

Day 3: Automated follow up e-mail in X days that appends original e-mail to bottom

Day 3: Engage with prospect's LinkedIn content

Day 3: LinkedIn InMail

Day 5: Phone call with voice mail

Day 6: Automated follow-up e-mail in X days that appends previous two e-mails to bottom

Day 10: Engage with prospect's LinkedIn content

Day 10: Customized e-mail written by rep

Day 10: Phone call

Day 13: Send branded swag

Day 16: LinkedIn connection request

And so on...We usually will make 18 to 20 touches within three to four weeks.

We set up this sequence one time in Outreach and then reps use it each day with new prospects they find in their accounts. This methodology allows our reps to focus on adding more prospects into the system and completing activities the sequence generates for them (many activities, because they are automated, are performed without the effort or attention of a sales rep). Because reps know what to personalize and how it should be done, and because we limit their activity to only personalized tasks, we are able to dramatically boost e-mail quality and quantity at the same time. Practice makes perfect, and we have reps practicing only the most important activities.

Here's the key to it all: If a response e-mail is received or a phone call is answered, our software knows this means you want to stop the process, so no future messaging/activity is generated for that prospect until the rep decides what to do next with the e-mail in their inbox or after they hang up the phone.

The Outreach Sales Process for Balancing E-mail Quality and Quantity

For optimum productivity plus a balance of e-mail quality and quantity, set up a clear process for your sales team that leverages workflow, research, and sales automation. This gives your company a clear advantage over the competition.

In order to master the impossible task of balancing e-mail quality and quantity, you have to build a muscle for it. People don't just write really great e-mails really fast. We have to help them develop that muscle.

The way that we do that at Outreach is through repetition and practice by using the Pomodoro method combined with coaching. The Pomodoro technique is a time management method developed by Francesco Cirillo in the late 1980s. The technique uses a timer to break down work into intervals, traditionally 25 minutes in length, separated by short breaks.

Set a timer for 25 minutes. The rep does a task, and only that task, for those 25 minutes. After the timer goes off, set the timer for 5 minutes to record your production, review the results, take a break, talk about who did great/who needs help, trade advice, up-vote best practices, etc. Repeat.

For example, spend 25 minutes writing custom e-mails. The first 25 minutes, you might write three e-mails; then the next 25-minute block, two e-mails; then the next, four e-mails; then the next, six e-mails; and so forth. Through repetition, a level of competency is developed, and mastery is earned. The key is identifying what leads to larger numbers in a period and working on getting great at those skills and techniques.

Reps will get faster at writing high-quality e-mails. Practice makes perfect, so give your team a way to practice. Through this method, you can coach your team on all aspects of the process, not just e-mails. Make more dials, research faster on LinkedIn, look for accounts that need more love, get to "the ask" quicker, find better trigger events, etc.

Here's a great story that characterizes the types of improvements and culture you can create with Pomodoro. Early on at Outreach, some of our SDRs were phone-averse. I am not. One of my first sales jobs was selling credit cards over the phone in college (yes, I was one of those horrible telemarketers). At that job, I would make 100 dials per hour (yes, per hour), and I would make about two sales per hour. That is 98 "no"s, "quit calling me"s, "I hate you"s, and "you suck"s per hour. You grow a thick skin at a job like that. You learn the phone is like an ATM: If you would only push the buttons, money will come out. I organized a week of 3-hour Pomodoro sessions for cold calling.

The team would start at 9 am for the first 25-minute block. We put a timer on a monitor at the front of the room. And to make it really fun, without telling them beforehand, I jumped right in the middle of them, grabbed a group of accounts, and started dialing. The average person punched out three phone calls in the first 25 minutes. I did 12. The next 5-minute block, they did eight, and I did 11. By the end of the first day, everyone was doing at least 10 calls per 25-minute block. We removed the fear, we found out workflows that held them back, and we celebrated our improvement. By the end of the week, nobody was scared of the phone, and we increased our dials per day by five times.

Companies that write the most high-quality e-mails (or whatever kind of task) will always outperform companies that can't execute as well or as fast. So if you want to have a competitive advantage, you need to make sure your team is equipped with tools and methods that give them an advantage.

I know this process and our product has given my team an advantage. We are sending out hundreds of e-mails a week that, as a group, garner reply rates of 25% or more. Imagine building a sales machine that could take 100 cold, outbound prospects and, in a week or two, get 25 of them to engage. That's legendary status—which is attainable to those trained and equipped correctly. Balancing e-mail quality and quantity can do that for you too.

There is no silver bullet for sequences. It's something you'll have to A/B test and always treat as a work in progress. However, there are some basic best practices.

- **The best time of day to send**. Based on data from 1.3 million e-mails, there are actually three best times to send that all yield a more than 40% reply rate: Mondays between 3 and 4 pm PT (43%), Mondays between 4 and 5 pm PT (42%), and Thursdays between 4 and 5 pm PT (41%).

- **The 5-minute rule**. No, this does not pertain to how long you can still eat a Frito that's fallen on the floor. It is actually a goldmine tip for reaching executives. The best time to call is at the 55-minute mark on the hour, because it's most likely when an exec has finished early from their previous meeting. If you call at the 15-minute mark, they will likely still be in the meeting.

- **Voice mail hook**. When leaving a voice mail, hit them with the hook first, not your name or company. Name of company first screams sales pitch and will get quickly deleted before they listen further. Get them hooked, then finish with the name, company, and number, all repeated two times.

- **Warm texts only**. Texting or SMS messaging is useful with the caveat that you have already established a relationship. Using it to confirm a meeting or get the contract back are great uses. Pulling the number from the Internet and texting them without first establishing a relationship is not a great idea.

- **Optimize the buyer's journey**. If you do get in touch, it might be a good idea to ask how they usually like to stay in touch. This way, you can note it in your CRM or SEP and use that method most going forward.

- **Stakeholder scope**. Another great thing to ask is, "Who else at your company should I involve in further communications?" This way, you can stop your other sequences and focus on the right key stakeholders.

- **Don't be close-hungry**. Often, your goal isn't to close the deal; it's to get the next meeting. Remember that!

For more Sales Engagement best practices, visit Outreach.io/blog.

There's another force at play when you do a sequence: It's called Effective Frequency. It's an age-old advertising term that refers to the number of times it takes for the buyer to see your brand in order to recognize or remember your company. When you do a sequence right, you can develop this pattern of Effective Frequency.

Although there are many microinsights above, the macroinsight is clear: Different buyer personas prefer different mediums and messaging techniques.

The takeaway? To move the business needle, you need to do the following:

- Educate your buyers via the medium they prefer.
- Meet your buyers via the channel they prefer.
- Engage them with tailored messaging that matters in their context. Be relevant, be personalized, and do it at scale.

Here are some tactical steps that will help align your strategy with the modern buying experience:

1. Get with your Marketing teams and test the different mediums like peer-review sites, forums, e-books, and others. In many cases, you can join these forums and become a trusted advisor or subject matter expert yourself.

As Jennifer Brandenburg, Vice President of Worldwide Inside Sales at GE Digital and Outreach customer, tells us, "The greatest advantage of a Sales Engagement Platform is that, because they enable a multi-touch strategy, you as a rep have the unequaled opportunity to build your brand as a salesperson! As you execute a flawless and thoughtful outreach campaign, you demonstrate your core company values. By providing targeted strategic communication to your prospect that they might find valuable, you have shown them that you are credible and have done your research on your key differentiators. In turn, this makes you a thought leader and trusted advisor in the eyes of your prospect."

2. Equip reps and Account Managers with a full range of content, personas, and messaging assets for them to successfully engage different customer personas at different points of the buyer journey. Then A/B test religiously. Test channels, test content—test where you can to improve.

3. Invest in an effective SEP that complements your team's creativity and drive with the speed, scope, and scale that allow them to execute omnichannel sequences flawlessly, thanks to powerful machine learning and data science.

Nail this and you're on your way to a modern, efficient Sales Engagement strategy. In our next chapter, we double-down on adding science to the sales process and show you how to take omnichannel outreach and sequences to the next level.

For more best practices on omnichannel sequences, including common myths busted, Sales Engagement best practices for down-funnel activities, and preparing for GDPR, visit Outreach.io/resources.

Chapter 5

Why A/B Testing Is Mission-critical to Any Sales Org

By now, you know that when we think about modern sales, we are talking in large part about the science of sales. Like a scientific experiment, you should always be testing multiple variables in your Sales Engagement process.

Here are examples of what you can start testing and what it can do for you:

- You can test subject line copy to learn which e-mail gets the best open rates.
- You can test subject line length to learn which e-mail gets the best open rates.
- You can test variations of your call to action to learn which link, call scheduling tactic, or copy results in more positive replies.
- You can test voice mail scripts to learn which messages work best.

When it comes to the science of sales, these test ideas are just the tip of the analytics iceberg. The possibilities for A/B testing your sales hypotheses are literally endless. For further A/B testing examples and advice, let's turn things over to Pavel Dmitriev, Vice President of Data Science at Outreach.

The Case for A/B Testing: Bing, a Few Lines of Code, and a $100 Million Annual Increase in Revenue

A 2017 issue of *Harvard Business Review* contained an interesting story. An engineer at Bing proposed a simple code change to the way ad headlines were displayed.[1] Through A/B testing, the company was amazed to learn that the change increased revenue by 12%—more than $100 million annually. That's the good news.

The bad news? There was a 6-month lag between the original idea being proposed and the actual implementation. This lag cost Bing more than $50 million in revenue.

The moral of the story? This was the best revenue-generating idea in Bing's history, no question. But because the team did not view the idea as very promising, it was neither tested nor implemented quickly; it was languishing in the backlog. Simply put, this was one expensive oversight.

Desperately Seeking Data: Why the Traditional Sales Playbook Is Fundamentally Flawed

What are the takeaways here? First, we all have brilliant ideas on how to improve the product, the sales process, the way we work, etc. Second, it is often hard to have our ideas heard and appreciated by others. That's why so many of our brilliant ideas never see the light of day. And when it

---

[1] https://hbr.org/2017/09/the-surprising-power-of-online-experiments

comes to the sales industry, the prevalence of antiquated sales playbooks almost guarantees they never will.

Sales orgs regularly forsake innovation for tradition, aka their tried-and-true playbooks. Well, these playbooks might be tried, but they are not necessarily true. Although there are exceptions, many sales playbooks today are still based on gut instinct, anecdotes, and individual experiences, rather than scientifically tested strategies.

Think about it: How do these plays come about? On a certain day, someone tried a certain template or a certain phrase in their e-mail. They got a reply, told others, and boom! Soon everyone started using it, and just like that, a new play was added to the playbook. If others are doing it, it must work, right? Not necessarily.

To make matters worse, when a sales executive moves to another company, they bring their myths and anecdotes with them—often into a completely different industry—and put them into their new playbook. Even if the idea worked well before, which itself is far from given, it is not likely those insights will be transferable to a new industry, persona, target market, etc.

So, you see, this bittersweet Bing case study above is not an isolated incident. Our research shows that sales reps, just like the enterprising Bing engineer, also have many ideas on how to improve playbooks. But convincing sales executives to try the ideas is often hard. Executives have years of experience, and it is hard for young reps to speak out and suggest that their ideas may be better than those of the sales leader.

And sales executives are not the villains of the story either. Unlike all other executive roles, sales executives live and die on the quarter. One can understand why sales executives are afraid to try new and risky ideas. If the idea does not work, it may very well cause them to miss their number, potentially costing them their jobs. No wonder they cling to their playbooks so closely.

Without a low-risk, quick way of testing new approaches, what options do they really have?

Objecting to Conventional Wisdom Around Objections

No wonder sales reps do not like playbooks and often do not follow them. In a case study with Glassdoor's sales team, we were looking to identify what the top-performing sales reps did different from the bottom-performing reps. One of the findings was that the top-performing reps replied to objections from customers *with the same urgency as to positive replies.* You guessed it—this practice deviated from the playbook, which recommended prioritizing positive replies and deprioritizing objections.

Bottom-performing reps, on the other hand, followed the playbook and replied to objections later or not at all and, as a result, performed poorly.

A Sales Problem Is a Company Problem

The matter is not a small one. A sales team's performance is often what determines whether the company succeeds or fails, whether the product gains critical mass or dies. Who knows? There could be a single idea like the Bing revelation in your organization right now. Whether it gets recognized and implemented or languishes on the backlog could be the difference between your department, or even business, thriving or going belly-up.

A/B Testing: The Critical Ingredient for a Modern Sales Playbook

But what if there were another way? What if we could organize the sales process so that everyone's ideas were heard and tried, bad ideas were quickly dropped, and good ones were adopted, creating a virtuous cycle of continuous performance improvement for the sales team? That is the sales exec's dream world. Does it exist? My answer is an astounding "Yes!" and A/B testing is the way to get there.

Examples: A/B Testing and Real Results

OK, you've heard me ramble about the importance of A/B testing for long enough. Let's look at the results from four real-world tests that we ran across different Sales Engagement interactions.

Before running any test, two things need to be defined: the hypothesis and the success criteria for the test. After the test is completed, the results are analyzed and a decision is made with respect to these criteria. Let's walk through these steps for our four examples.

Test 1: Tough Sell Versus Soft Sell

In sales, the conventional wisdom is that the more aggressive bird gets the worm. But is that actually the case? Or a stereotype? Let's find out.

> **Hypothesis:** Soft sell will work better at later stages of the sequence—after several attempts to contact the prospect already failed.
>
> **Success criteria:** Increase in positive reply rate.

Template A

Subject: Sales pain points/quick call?

Hey {{first_name}},

In short, we're a sales automation platform that makes your reps' lives a lot easier. Our average companies (based on 1,100 + companies) have tripled their reply rates on cold outbound e-mails and boosted rep productivity by 2X.

We take what your best reps are doing and automate that across your entire team so your weaker reps can work at the highest possible same level. We also solve the issue of follow-up falling through the cracks and reps not going deep enough.

When can I get a few minutes on your calendar to discuss?

{{sender.first_name}}

Template B

Subject: Quick call next week?

{{first_name}},

I'm sure in your role you get a ton of sales-driven e-mails, probably most of which are spam you have no interest in. My goal is to provide enough value to warrant a 15-minute call with you.

What we do is put your sales process into a structured series of touch-points, which takes care of your follow-up process for you. This ramps up reps' activities and ensures that every lead is thoroughly worked, never gets lost, and receives the five to 12 touches where 80% of sales happen.

Second, we do all the administrative work for you in your CRM (Salesforce). This frees up your reps' time, logs their activities, and gives you 100% accurate reporting.

Finally, we open up the "Black Box" of sales and show you in real time how each rep is performing, what activities they're doing, and what is and isn't working. This provides a solid foundation to accurately forecast results, improve your outreach, and train your team.

Over 1,100 companies (like CenturyLink, Adobe, and Marketo) use us, and their average rep saves 2 hours a day and 2X their productivity.

If you see value here, can we set up a time next Tuesday or Wednesday to discuss?

{{sender.first_name}}

Answer: Template A had about a 70% higher reply rate. The vast majority of the replies, however, were negative or unsubscribe requests. Template B, though it had a lower reply rate, had about a 40% higher overall positive reply rate.

Our analysis: All reply rates are not created equal. Although the aggressive e-mail was more successful at provoking a response, the response it provoked was negative. The softer approach had fewer replies—that is, fewer people replying angrily to unsubscribe—but the response of those who opened was significantly more positive. Remember: The goal is to further the deal, not just get a reply. Therefore, the softer sell is more successful.

Test 2: Longer Versus Shorter E-mails

It is said that today's consumers have shorter attention spans than ever. Therefore, a shorter communication will be more successful. True or untrue? Let's find out.

> **Hypothesis:** Shorter e-mails will be more effective.
> **Success criteria:** Positive reply rate.

Template A

Hey {{first_name}},

Just checking in again.

Can you give me a thumbs up or thumbs down on whether you are interested?

Best,

{{sender.first_name}}

Template B

Hey {{first_name}},

Just checking in again.

Ultimately, there are four main things that Outreach will help you accomplish:

- Increase activity, which will increase opportunities and revenue (the way we've helped Cloudera).
- Save the average rep about 2 hours a day (as Bizible has seen).
- Create a predictable consistent model that gets your weakest rep to perform at the highest level (as Datanyze has experienced).
- Track and measure what works (like NextWorks).

Can you give me a thumbs up or thumbs down on whether you are interested?

Best,

{{sender.first_name}}

Answer: Not only does Template A have a 239% higher reply rate than Template B (13.9% versus 4.1%) at a 99% confidence level, but Template A also generates a higher proportion of positive replies (8.9% versus 6.3%) and a lower unsubscribe rate (7.1% versus 12.5%). It is the all-around winner.

Our analysis: Shorter is definitely sweeter! This test also shows how piling on the salesy language and name-dropping does not lead to success. Keep it short, keep it sincere, and keep it human.

Test 3: LinkedIn Mention Versus No LinkedIn Mention

Is LinkedIn really queen when it comes to sales communication mediums? That is the assumption of most salespeople, but let's find out if it's actually true.

> **Hypothesis:** Sales rep mentioning that he looked at the prospect's information on LinkedIn will increase effectiveness of the e-mail.
>
> **Success criteria:** Positive reply rate.

Template A

Hi {{first_name}},

I noticed that you've been in sales leadership for quite some time. Given our customers in your space, you will find this relevant.

I work for Outreach, a Sales Engagement Platform. It's our goal to mold to your sales processes and streamline them to make you and your team more efficient and productive.

For example, Lars Nilsson, Cloudera's VP of Global Inside Sales, needed a solution for his team to consistently follow up on leads. Here is how he increased his team's meetings set by 54%, solved his issue, and upped their reply rate by 10X.[2]

Would next week work for you to discuss?

Best,

{{sender.first_name}}

---

[2] https://www.outreach.io/why-outreach/case-studies/cloudera

Template B

Hi {{first_name}},

I saw on LinkedIn that you've been in sales leadership for quite some time. Given our customers in your space, you will find this relevant.

I work for Outreach, an enterprise communication platform for sales. It's our goal to mold to your sales processes and streamline them to make you and your team more efficient and productive.

For example, Lars Nilsson, Cloudera's VP of Global Inside Sales, needed a solution for his team to consistently follow up on leads. Here is how he increased his team's meetings set by 54%, solved his issue, and upped their reply rate by 10X.

Would next week work to discuss?

Best,

{{sender.first_name}}

Answer: Template A has a 25% higher reply rate than Template B at a 95% confidence level. Before we established reply intent detection capability, we concluded that Template A was more effective than Template B. Accounting for intent, however, Template B had a higher overall positive reply rate.

Our analysis: This test echoed the refrain from the tough sell versus soft sell test. Although Template B had a lower open and reply rate, of the people that *did* open that e-mail, their sentiment was more positive. This makes sense: The people who opened this e-mail knew it was a cold outreach and were open to it. There may be fewer of those people, but those who did open knew what they were getting.

Using "I noticed that…" as an introduction got more opens and replies, but fewer positive ones, because it feels like more of a bait and switch. Someone who opens this e-mail is probably expecting to see a mutual contact or at least some more personalized content. Because the body of the e-mail delivers neither, it's not surprising that the prospect gets a bad taste in their mouth and rejects the e-mail.

Sales Engagement #gotyourback Pro Tip

"Remember, while low open rates aren't fun, there is nothing worse than an unsubscribe—there is no coming back from that!"

—*Pavel Dmitriev, Vice President of Data Science at Outreach*

Test 4: "Just Checking in"

It's one of the biggest rules in sales. Never say "just checking in" unless you want to repel your prospect. But is it true? Let's find out what the data says.

> **Hypothesis:** Mentioning "just checking in" in a sales e-mail reduces e-mail effectiveness.
>
> **Success criteria:** Increased reply rate.

Template A: No "Just Checking in"

Hi {{first_name}},

Making sure my last note reached your inbox. I know things can get lost and I wanted to get back on your radar.

When can I get a few minutes on your calendar to talk?

Thanks,

{{sender.first_name}}

Template B: Added "Just Checking In"

Hi {{first_name}},

Just checking in.

Making sure my last note reached your inbox. I know things can get lost and I wanted to get back on your radar.

When can I get a few minutes on your calendar to talk?

Thanks,

{{sender.first_name}}

Answer: Adding "Just checking in" (Template B) resulted in an 86% increase in reply rate.

Our analysis: Trust me; this one shocked us too. This was contrary to the expectation of everyone in the sales org. The popular belief in sales circles for decades is that "just checking in" never works.

Here is one important caveat though: "Just checking in" worked better *in this context*. There were other scenarios where it did not work as well.

Although there are many micro-ahas in the previous examples, the big aha is this: There are no silver bullets. There are many nuances in data that make all the difference. Although we may wish for a silver bullet to make life easy, it is important to dig in and really understand the details and the right metrics, lest you make a cavalier snap decision that won't actually increase performance.

For more analysis, content, and quizzes, visit salesengagement.com/abtesting.

The Metrics That Matter (and Ones That Don't)

Reply rates are important, but they don't tell the whole story. Based on an analysis from 100,000 e-mails, Outreach Amplify, Outreach's machine learning engine, found that simply measuring reply rate is not a sufficient sales metric.

We know—this feels like sales sacrilege. If someone responds, that's good, right? But the reality is not all replies are created equal.

Case in point: Any sales rep who's ever gotten an e-mail that looks like this will tell you that not all replies are created equally:

Subject: RE: EXAMPLESOFT
Reply: Unsubscribe me right now or else!!!

Yes, the reply rate you get is a huge indicator of engagement with your e-mails. But that's Sales and Marketing 101. If you want to truly drive next-level results, the most important thing for you to measure is the quality of your replies, not just the quantity. Let's dig deeper.

In sales, every reply to an outbound e-mail will essentially fall into one of three categories:

Unsubscribes: You're completely out of the running here. You legally cannot continue to cold e-mail this prospect or you will be out of compliance with CAN-SPAM laws. This is the one reply you don't want in your inbox.

Objections: Your prospect replied to your e-mail only to let you know that they don't have budget. Ideal? No. But with the right strategy, can you turn this into a deeper conversation? You bet. Although it's not the ideal scenario, there's still opportunity in an objection. Remember the Glassdoor case study we discussed above— an objection is still better than radio silence.

Positive replies: This is the magical reply that goes something like, "Funny you should e-mail me because I was just thinking there has to be a better solution than what I'm doing today. When can we meet?" BOOM! Everything you do should be optimizing for this reaction.

Ultimately, you want to maximize the number of e-mails with positive intent you receive. That's why simply measuring reply rate won't cut it. What if you get a 50% reply rate and 40% are unsubscribes? If you measure only the reply rate without digging into the details, you will be sending a prospect-repelling e-mail out at full force. What you need your sales e-mail metrics to measure is reply quality *as well as quantity.*

The solution: Measure reply intent in conjunction with reply rate.

Through Outreach's machine learning program, Amplify, we were able to gain a new level of insight into our top-performing e-mails, seeing not only what drove replies but also what drove positive reply intent.

How to Shine a Light on the Prospect That's Gone Dark

A common problem sales reps are always trying to solve is how to tactfully nudge a prospect who has gone dark without being annoying. We tested three e-mails to try and figure out the best way to do this.

If you were optimizing for reply rate only, you would have chosen to use Template 1, which provided a reply rate of 6.1%. However, 20% of those replies were unsubscribes, which means you just lost those prospects forever.

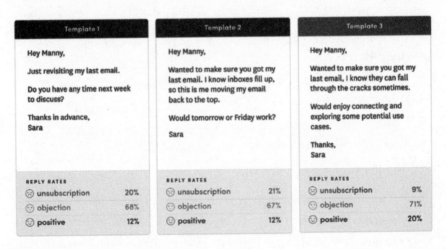

Figure 5.1   Attempting to Nudge a Prospect

When you dig a little deeper and look at the intent of the replies, you'll see that in fact Template 3 was the most successful in generating positive replies (which, depending on your team, can convert tens of times better than objections) and very effective at minimizing unsubscribes. In fact, Template 3's positive reply rate was almost twice as high (70% higher to be exact) than the next best performer, Template 1.

Multiply that out over 1,000 e-mails and optimizing for positive replies in this case would leave you with seven fewer unsubscribes and three more positive interactions with a higher likelihood of conversion. And that's just one step in one sequence!

Think of all the qualified meetings and future happy customers you could be leaving on the table if you're not optimizing for conversations your prospects actually want to have.

Other Areas to A/B Test

We just went long and hard on A/B testing via e-mail engagement, but what about other channels?

E-mail is still king, with about 70% of sales communication happening over e-mail, but other channels are the future. Our Data Science team is working on adding A/B testing to more channels both natively supported and enabled through our partners—companies like:

- Video: Vidyard, Videolicious, OneMob, Brightcove, VidGrid, BombBomb, etc.
- Calls: Gong, Chorus, Avoma, ExecVision, etc.
- Direct mail: Sendoso, PFL, Kotis, etc.
- Chat: Drift, Intercom, LivePerson, etc.
- Sales collateral: DocSend, Highspot, Showpad, etc.
- And many more

For an in-depth discussion of A/B testing in sales, the most promising aspects to test, and how to organize the testing program within your organization to keep continuously improving your sales process, visit salesengagement.com/abtesting.

Chapter 6

Achieving Revenue Efficiency: Metrics to Measure in a Modern Sales Org

Now that we've taken you through humanizing your message at scale, building omnichannel sequences, and A/B testing it all, we really need to make sure we're measuring the right metrics to hit optimal sales and Revenue Efficiency.

If you are familiar with real estate, you might have heard the term *highest and best use*. This is an important concept in determining the value of real estate. The highest and best use of a property or building is the use that achieves maximum possible productivity and, therefore, profit. Sales Efficiency is the same idea applied to sales teams.

In order to create a truly efficient sales program, leadership must constantly ask: "Is this the highest and best use of my sales rep's time and energy?" This approach to sales can mean the difference between a starving sales team and a revenue machine.

Your definition of *efficient* is based largely on your goals. No two teams will define Sales Efficiency exactly the same way. A sales program focused on a small number of high-value accounts (Account-based Sales Development [ABSD]) will define efficiency differently than a team fielding thousands of transactional inbound leads every month. However, there are a few elements of Sales Efficiency that transcend Go-to-Market (GTM) strategies.

A perfectly efficient sales org allows reps to spend their time on three activities:

- Choosing targets (companies or people)
- Talking to new prospects
- Nurturing old prospects

Although Sales Efficiency may feel like a nebulous concept, that's only because most leaders have never been shown how to measure their sales funnel. In this chapter, we will teach you how to do it.

By the end of this chapter, you'll know how to confidently answer the question that makes sales leaders nervous: "What resources do you need to deliver $X of new pipeline next quarter?" This will allow you to deliver more revenue and forecast more accurately as it compounds over time.

Today, we'll focus specifically on efficiency as it relates to outbound pipeline development programs with large Total Addressable Markets (TAMs), which describes most teams focused on Sales Engagement.

In order to do it justice (pun intended—you'll see why), we brought in our longtime customer and friend Taft Love. Taft started his career as a police officer and detective before moving over to run Sales and Pipeline Development for multiple hypergrowth companies (maybe that explains why his teams are so good at prospecting). He previously led Sales Development at SmartRecruiters and is currently the VP of Pipeline and Marketing Operations at HouseCanary. Taft's first step? Better understand your pipeline.

Taft's Take: Understanding Your Pipeline

Achieving Pipeline Efficiency (an important component of Revenue Efficiency) begins with understanding your Sales Development funnel.

Ask any experienced VP of Sales about their Account Executives' (AEs') funnel, and they can rattle off all sorts of metrics. Close rate, win rate, average deal size, sales cycle length, etc. They know these metrics because it's their job.

Companies understand why these metrics are so important. Sales organizations invest heavily in Operations teams that help them identify, track, and trust their funnel metrics. But few companies give much thought to understanding their Sales Development funnel.

Most Sales Development leaders aren't expected to know their funnel metrics like the VP of Sales—yet. However, the landscape is shifting rapidly for Sales Development leaders, and knowing your funnel will not be rare within a year or two. Achieving Revenue Efficiency is simply not possible if you can manage—and therefore measure—only the top half of your funnel.

This section will focus on showing you exactly how to capture the metrics that Sales Development leaders need to understand their funnel like a VP of Sales would.

To be clear, knowing open and response rates of e-mails is not the same as understanding your funnel.[1] Sales Development leaders often use these ratios in place of an actual funnel because they are easy to measure. Most e-mail automation tools have shallow reporting capabilities that end at the activity level, but new, more robust technologies like SEPs can measure all the way to revenue attribution. It's 2019—is anyone still investing in software solutions that don't measure down to the dollar?

Sales Development funnels are more difficult to measure than AE funnels for two reasons:

---

[1] https://www.outreach.io/blog/understanding-your-sales-development-funnel

1. In most teams, no two SDRs prospect exactly the same way.
2. The AE funnel is tracked within a single object (opportunity), but the Sales Development funnel is spread across four (contact, account, task, opportunity).

This represents a huge problem for data-driven teams. If you don't know your Sales Development funnel, you can't accurately forecast the resources necessary to deliver pipeline. You can guess, and you may even get it right sometimes, but guessing gets harder as you grow.

In order to understand your funnel, there are two things you need to do:

1. Reconcile your two Sales Development funnels: activities and accounts.
2. Build a system for measuring your funnel.

Taft's Take: Standardizing Your Sales Development Funnel

I recently spoke with a Sales Development leader who knew she needed additional headcount to hit upcoming goals but had no idea how to justify it to her executive team. She knew instinctively that her current team of about a dozen SDRs wouldn't be able to hit the next quarter's pipeline goal, but she just couldn't justify it using hard metrics.

Roughly a quarter of her SDRs conducted all their outbound prospecting via LinkedIn. Of the remaining reps, most relied primarily on e-mail while a few hit the phones hard. This inconsistency led to a few reps crushing their goals with the rest struggling to keep up. She found it impossible to gauge the skill level of reps based on their performance when they all employed different strategies. That doesn't scale.

This is a common story in SDR-land. Few teams have built the infrastructure necessary to connect effort to outcomes. Instead, they rely exclusively on metrics like e-mail open and response rates that tell only part of the story.

Until recently, Sales Development has not had a seat at the proverbial table, so the pressure to provide data to back up strategic decisions has not existed. However, this is changing as more and more Sales Development leaders—myself included—report directly to C-level executives (usually the Chief Revenue Officer [CRO] or Chief Executive Officer [CEO]).

There are two simple steps to understanding and measuring your Sales Development funnel:

1. Clearly define how accounts and contacts enter your funnel.
2. Use outbound automation to ensure every account requires the same amount of effort to move it through the funnel.

Define the Top of Your Funnel

Clearly defining what it means for a prospect to enter the funnel is a must. For the Sales Development team at SmartRecruiters (a team I built and led), we created a concept called *activation*. Once an account or contact is activated, they have entered our outbound Sales Development funnel.

The definitions of activation for contacts and accounts are clear and simple. This makes them easy to understand and track within Salesforce:

A contact is activated when it is:	An account is activated when it is:
- Marked as an outbound target contact in Salesforce	- Marked as an outbound target account in Salesforce
AND	AND
- Added to an outbound sequence in Outreach.io	- Six contacts in the account are activated
AND	
- At least two activities have been logged against the contact in Salesforce	

For keeping track of activation, we use a tool called Rollup Helper.[2] It allows us to automatically mark accounts and contacts as activated and get other valuable insights via Salesforce reports.

Standardize Outbound Effort

Now that you know what it means for a company to enter your outbound funnel, the next step is to create a template for outbound prospecting that is applied to every target. I use the word *template* because the messaging and content can change, but the number and types of activities should always remain the same.

In order to make sure that reps adhere to the outbound template, we use sequences in Outreach. A sequence is a series of touchpoints (activities) that are managed within Outreach to ensure that reps follow up at predetermined intervals. One of our sequences is our activity template. It is a blank sequence that serves as a skeleton into which we add content.

Consistent follow-up is only part of the value of sequences. Sequences are also a great way to control the resources required for a prospect to move through your funnel.

Knowing the amount of activities each account activation requires makes resource planning possible. Only when you know what an activation costs in terms of bandwidth, you can reconcile your two funnels (accounts and activities).

Understanding the funnel metrics is important, but that knowledge is valuable only if you can measure every piece of your funnel. Guessing the metrics is a mistake. Proper planning requires understanding the average numbers across both of your funnels.

Understanding what's really happening in your Sales Development activity funnel is especially important. Just because your template has

---

[2] https://www.passagetechnology.com/rollup-helper-overview

20 activities doesn't mean that every prospect will receive 20 touches. Prospects fall out of your funnel for lots of reasons—they may respond to your outreach, agree to a meeting, or opt out midsequence.

Building the infrastructure necessary to track everything can be challenging, but your Operations team (or a qualified consultant) can help you build reporting to understand exactly what is happening in your funnel. Plus, you can check out my real life examples! Check out the information at the end of this chapter.

Once you have a dashboard in place that accurately displays the various ratios that make up your funnel, you can begin to plan resources to increase efficiency.

The Impact of Increased Efficiency

Once you understand your Sales Development funnel, it becomes possible to understand the value of each activity, which is something that most teams have never been able to do. Now you can put a dollar amount on the opportunity cost of having your Sales Development team focus on anything other than selling.

Take a moment and think about what your SDRs' days look like. Some of the most famous Sales Development programs in tech ask their SDRs to do low-skill work that could be outsourced to lower-cost teams.

According to a 2018 survey conducted by HubSpot, the average salesperson spends less than 36% of their day prospecting. Another 46% is spent finding leads, gathering contact information, writing e-mails, and doing other activities that SDRs should not be doing.

Let's use the fake company EXAMPLESOFT.com to demonstrate the difference that a small bump in efficiency can make. Although the following metrics are made up, they are all in the normal range for most outbound Sales Development programs.

EXAMPLESOFT

- Four outbound SDRs
- 100 activities per activated account (on average)
- 5% of activated accounts move to pipeline
- $50,000 average deal size
- 30% close rate on deals that enter pipeline

Let's assume that by spending 36% of their day prospecting, each SDR at EXAMPLESOFT.com is able to activate three new accounts each day (that was the early expectation at SmartRecruiters). That means the team activates 240 new accounts each month.

In this scenario, each SDR generates $150K in new outbound pipeline each month. Based on San Francisco SDR compensation, this team is probably generating 10 times its cost in pipeline each month. That's good enough to justify the team's existence but not particularly impressive.

Now let's look at what would happen if we applied the same funnel metrics to a team that is able to use their time more efficiently. Let's assume that, instead of adding three new accounts to their Sales Development funnel every day, each SDR adds five new accounts.

For the team at EXAMPLESOFT.com, enabling SDRs to add two additional accounts into their Sales Development funnel every day rockets the team from $600K to $1M in new pipeline each month. Even more significant improvement is possible when leaders apply the highest and best concept to their Sales Development programs.

I've heard countless Sales Development leaders say some version of the following: "I suppose I could outsource some low-skill activities, but that's just part of their job. SDRs have a healthy base salary for that reason."

This mentality costs Sales Development programs incredible amounts of money. Every hour spent doing something other than selling—like finding and verifying contact information for prospects—is far costlier than most leaders realize.

Using the examples above, we can put an actual number on this. Let's say that the average activity takes 1 minute to complete (it's actually less in real life as most activities are automated e-mails). In both the previous examples, the value of an activity is about $8. That means that the opportunity cost of a high-performance SDR doing anything other than selling is $480 per hour ($8 × 60 minutes). This doesn't even include what you're paying them!

The first step to take when trying to achieve true Pipeline Efficiency is to look at every single activity that makes up your Sales Development process. For each activity, ask these two simple questions:

1. Is this activity so complex that a lower-cost resource couldn't do it effectively?
2. Will outsourcing this activity negatively impact their development as sales reps?

If the answer to both questions is "no," then you shouldn't burden your Sales Development team with it.

At SmartRecruiters, the added efficiency was so valuable that we ultimately created a Sales Development Operations team whose sole focus was making sure that SDRs did the smallest number of non-selling activities possible. We gutted their process, removing every step between choosing a target account and making the first phone call.

The average sales rep uses six tools as part of their prospecting process (I suspect the number is higher for SDRs), so we began by removing as many of those tools as possible. Thanks to the Sales Development Operations team, they ultimately needed three—LinkedIn, our CRM, and an SEP.

At our peak performance, the Sales Development team tripled the number of accounts they added to their funnel each month AND improved the team's funnel metrics—likely a result of more talk time and less boring lead research time.

Now it's time for you to get started finding ways to make your Sales Development team more efficient, starting where I did by taking a close look at every single activity your SDRs do each day and finding ways to remove any non-selling activities.

Want to see the actual examples Taft created to build his legendary funnel? Go to salesengagement.com/sdrfunnel.

Chapter 7

The Key to Ramping New Reps Faster

An underrated aspect of a strong Sales Engagement strategy is the ability to ramp reps much faster than ever before. Ramping starts with process above all. Without a repeatable, replicable process, it's almost impossible to ramp or forecast ramp time of new reps.

A solid Sales Engagement strategy not only allows for the creation of an easy and controlled process, but it also provides the necessary metrics and oversight to train and coach best practices that you are 100% sure are actually best practices.

As the leading Sales Engagement company, of course, we have something to say on the matter. We drink our own champagne and pride ourselves on being quick to ramp, making every quarter faster than the previous one. We cultivate a beginner's mindset.

So why let the execs talk when we could go straight to the source? Our seasoned SDR Manager, Sam Nelson, has ramped every new rep at Outreach for the past two years. This is his day in and day out at Outreach, so naturally it made sense for us to go to him to share his advice (and some if it was surprising, even to us!).

This is not only for companies that break out SDRs, AEs, and Customer Success Managers (CSMs) but also for companies that have full cycle reps that prospect, close deals, and upsell.

Sam's Take: The Four Traits of World-Class SDRs

- **Cash**
- **Ambitious**
- **Hard-working**
- **Shameless**

Good SDRs come in different shapes and sizes, but they rarely come without these attributes.

Despite an impressively tenured applicant pool, we have found that most of our top performers are recent grads or those who don't have any previous sales experience. SEPs have made it easier than ever to enter the SDR role and leverage the positive skill sets and qualities of Millennials.

The blank-slate candidate with the aforementioned qualities is surprisingly successful.

After trialing a variety of methods over many SDR onboarding classes, we've discovered the keys to ramping success:

1. Call-only sequences for the first two months.

SEPs *can* automate most of the non-selling activity in the prospecting process. In fact, if you take out calls and manual e-mails, you can create a sequence that is entirely automated and will provide some return.

Although there is a time and place for this strategy, you should avoid fully automated sequences during the first two months. The risk here is that SDRs use them and have some success and then make it foundational to their prospecting strategy. If this happens, the SDR will plateau quickly and be difficult to retrain. An SDR that cannot execute well on the phone will never reach their full potential. Even if they are the best sequencer/e-mailer in the world, any actual scheduling should be done over the phone. Cold outbound phone skills directly translate to an SDR's ability to convert e-mail meetings on the phone.

For these reasons, we allow SDRs to execute call sequences during the first two months only.

2. Give SDRs a holistic understanding in the first week.

Use the 80/20 rule here: 80% of results come from 20% of the effort. Focus on what's important. This is usually the script, the process for setting a meeting, the process for sequencing, and the correct titles to go after for each sequence. Keep sequences for new reps to 10 or fewer.

3. Have an SDR-specific boot camp.

The month we switched to an SDR-specific boot camp was our best first month for new hires of all time. If you do not currently have an SDR boot camp, you can probably get some quick returns by creating one. The challenge here will be to keep it focused on the fundamentals and skills that will be immediately applicable their first week. Teaching SDRs something that is valuable but not immediately necessary for them in that first week does more harm than good. There is only so much information they can take in, so be careful.

4. Implement new strategies with the new SDRs.

We have a specific team for the brand-new SDRs we call our Agoge. The name is inspired by Sparta's training camp for prospective warriors. By putting all new SDRs in the Agoge, we have seen a few advantages:

- By having a manager specialize in ramping new reps, you can ensure all new SDRs receive the same treatment.
- The SDR leader can specialize in ramping and master the challenges specific to new SDRs.
- If the Agoge leader was a top performer, the Agoge is a great place to replicate their strategies.
- The Agoge leader can eventually handle a high volume of brand-new SDRs. The capacity of this SDR manager will increase, and the capacity of the other managers (who no longer need to allocate bandwidth to ramping reps) increases as well.

- The Agoge allows larger companies to implement changes quickly and easily. New SDRs in the Agoge are the most likely to adopt new ideas from the manager, and you can see (in an environment where there is little downside if it fails) whether those ideas actually work. If they do, it is easy to get buy-in to implement them across the team.

5. Get SDRs comfortable with discomfort.

It is easy for sales leaders to forget how completely unnatural it is for someone who has not previously been in sales to "close." In the SDR's case, that means asking for the meeting. This behavior can feel awkward and will usually lead to rejection, which many SDRs are not used to. When SDRs first get on the phone, I tell them that there are three acceptable outcomes from every call: (i) a meeting, (ii) a hang-up, or (iii) a referral if they realize that they have called the wrong person. Do not be afraid to over-rotate on the importance of closing. It is much easier to ask SDRs to ease up on this than the other way around.

Brooke Bachesta, another of our seasoned Sales Development team leaders at Outreach, takes us a little deeper into making sure your ramping reps don't get stuck in the manual minutiae of prospecting.

Brooke's Take: My Evolving Adventures as an SDR

Back when I started as an SDR, it was a pure volume game. I was working for a tech startup in the Bay Area, and I remember when the unsubscribe button became a thing and we all panicked: "Who are we even going to talk to now?!"

As customers began to gain more control of their product buying cycles, sales teams were forced to pivot. We started to move away from the tried-and-true mass e-mail approach for several reasons, with perhaps the most notable being that customers were just plain tired of those tactics. With a wealth of information available via databases, review sites, and blogs, customers could answer a number of their own questions. It became clear that as SDRs, we were not pulling and pushing anymore; we were curating and cultivating a buying experience.

The plight of the SDR is a complex one. We have to be loud enough to cut through the rest of the noise but not upset our prospects. We have to spend enough time researching to be relevant while finding ways to spread our impact across hundreds of prospects at once. But how on earth do you do all that without losing out on time and revenue?

The prospecting rep has three likely time-burglar do's and don'ts that every Sales Manager *must* watch out for.

DON'T: Try Working Every Account Under the Sun

SDRs often feel like a Jack or Jane of all trades, master of none. This is because our focus is lost by a sneaky manual time suck: researching tons of different industries and verticals.

For example, if a rep is tasked with reaching out to micro and small and mid-sized businesses (SMB) and midmarket and commercial accounts, she'll likely have a hard time switching between workflows and research. A VP of Sales at a 10-person company likely has different concerns than one at a Fortune 100 company. How does that manifest in manual tasks, you might ask?

Let's quickly zoom in on manual steps on a micro account:

1. Check the account history in Salesforce.
2. Find the decision maker on LinkedIn.
3. Merge their data over from a contact database.
4. Draft an e-mail.
5. Put them in a touchpoint and move on to the next person.

This entire process takes about 15 minutes. The more of these they do, the faster they become at finding and reaching out to people. Scaling productivity comes from curating a second-nature ability to build accounts and reach out en masse with pointed, relevant nuggets of information. It's typically easier to do this in small accounts because I, as a rep, can use the laser vision LinkedIn provides to narrow in on my point of contact within minutes.

Now let's zoom in on the manual work in commercial accounts.

A commercial account, on the other hand, has several, if not dozens, of decision makers. An account with people and departments inherently comes with more complexity. So if you look at the manual steps on a commercial account, much more detail and planning are needed. In addition to all the tasks outlined for micro accounts, commercial accounts require the following fact checking/prep work:

1. Do we know anyone at the account?
2. Has the buyer worked with us before or at any of our customer companies?
3. Are they acquiring any of our partners?
   a. How about our competitors?
4. What's the best team to start with?
   a. What personas should we start with?
   b. Which geographic team of those do we start with?
   c. Do they all report to the same person or are there several regional VPs to involve?
   d. Is one team better positioned than the others to be our first customer? Should we leverage one for a foot in the door even if they're not an ideal customer?
5. Do we know who we should involve for procurement?
   a. Should we start reaching out now or later on down the deal?
6. Are we going to any events nearby where we can plan an in-person meeting? Should we start planning one?
7. What about all of the other details (title changes, language within the account/industry/prospect sales cycle, etc.) that comes up once an SDR starts researching?

This process requires clear partnership between the SDR, their AE, and oftentimes their executives. It could take days or weeks to unveil a clear working strategy.

The necessity to specialize is clear—arm your reps with the knowledge they need to funnel information and people and deals to the appropriate people and allow them the space to become hungry craftspeople and experts in their trade. Envision a world where you know that when your rep contacts a prospect, they're representing your company as the expert in "West Coast-based tech companies under 200 people that specialize in education management" rather than "the rep who was assigned to this account."

At my current company, we dedicate a team of two Senior SDRs to lead our efforts in prospecting into commercial and enterprise teams exclusively. To give you an idea of scale, one commercial rep drove $1.5 million in pipeline with 57 Sales Accepted Leads (SALs), whereas another of our successful SMB/midmarket reps drove $1.8 million with more than 100 SALs. We need the volume in the SMB space, but there's a clear difference in value per SAL with commercial. Also note that with commercial SALs, that pipeline value is just based on *initial* pipeline. The expansion value is often three to four or even five times that. So that $1.5 million in initial pipeline is really a potential $7.5 million with land and expand.

DO: Make Sure to Help Reps Prioritize

When observing new reps, how often have you thought to yourself as a manager, "Why did you just spend an hour doing this admin work when there are leads out there?!" New reps often struggle with a set of similar issues, and most of them stem from an inability to prioritize. It's a highly coachable trait, but most new reps treat each task with the same level of urgency. In an industry where you can be constantly busy but not always productive, it's more important than ever to have clear marching orders on a by-the-hour schedule.

Leaders should give reps a clear understanding of what order tasks should be completed in. We could make the case for a number of factors including engagement level, time to response, or size of account—it depends on your sales cycle and business. The important thing is to decide on a process, test it out, and then test some more.

What happens when this isn't clear to your reps? Imagine Jane at her desk. She's carefully alphabetized all her accounts to begin going through and qualifying them. She's made a spreadsheet that includes the size of the account and the number of buyers there. She's finding nuggets of information to reach out with for each account starting with ACME Incorporated and moving toward Zeppelin Enterprises.

What's wrong with this picture? Jane has no idea if ACME is better qualified than an account that starts with Q or R or S and has now spent hours and hours inputting data for accounts that have a low close rate.

How can we help Jane? Provide her with clear direction on the types of accounts she should focus on. Perhaps alphabetizing isn't the best way to sort. Maybe it's by market segment, or industry, or geolocation. She won't know unless her manager or another rep has told her that. And in the meantime, she's now started a chain of outreach to potentially unqualified accounts that will book a meeting in roughly three weeks, take up an hour on AEs' calendars, and result in a lost closed opportunity another week later. That entire month of productivity could have been geared toward better target accounts with statistically higher chances of closing.

DO: Codify the Constant Data Cleanup Loop and Encourage Reps to Ask for Help

How much time are your reps spending doing data cleanup? The occasional address change or the all-too-often mobile number update? This stuff takes time. And lots of it. Say you've got 1,000 prospects in your system. And for a quarter of those, there's an error in their name (maybe their name isn't capitalized), their number is out of service, or their title is off (Director of Sales versus Sales Director). Each time your rep manually updates that, that takes, what, 30 seconds? But then they have to remember to check for it on every contact, so add another 5 seconds. Then they may forget to fix it while they're in Google Chrome Tab-land

and then have to go back to it, breaking their workflow. Call it 37 seconds in total. That's 2.5 hours per rep spent fixing spelling errors. How big is your team? How often do you shuffle accounts and territories and managers and repeat the process of cleaning? This stuff—it adds up.

Who hates dirty CRM data? We do! And I'd bet you do too. Delegate this task to a team whose job it is to improve data quality. These are your unsung heroes of productivity. Behold: the Data Quality and Data Science teams! I can't stress enough how logistically helpful it is to have a squad of folks cleaning and then tidying and then ultimately maintaining our data. Bringing in unbiased parties and using data to drive decisions (groundbreaking, I know) is crazy helpful.

Allow yourself to spend your time coaching and observing and tweaking workflow. Allow your reps to spend time selling when you stop sucking up their time with tasks like requesting accounts, harvesting new contacts/accounts, cleaning up data, frankensteining e-mails, amending SFDC data, analyzing e-mail data, etc.

We're now selling in a market where reps are no longer spending their entire day writing one-off e-mails to individual prospects. They're running complex campaigns with templated outreach to multiple people in concert with Account Executives, Demand Gen, and Marketing. To give you a sense of scale, before modern sales technology, reps may have been able to manage around 50 people and talk tracks. Their calendars would be full of "don't forget to call so and so" and "remember to e-mail this account." But now, reps manage close to 500 people at a time. There's a constant ebb and flow of prospects coming in and out of the sales cycle with autocreated tasks.

We're inching closer and closer to a world where customers get the information they need when they need and want it, and reps are being positioned as Chief Networking Agents rather than cold callers. A large majority of the tedium mentioned above can be automated. Now more than ever, SDR managers need to leverage their tool stack and find ways to leverage their reps as salespeople, not sales activity machines. This is the key to ramping reps not only faster but also better.

SEPs also make it easier to compare activities between reps. Jennifer Brandenburg, Vice President of Worldwide Inside Sales at GE Digital, leverages data from Outreach for exactly that. Jennifer comments, "Leaders can quickly spot what top performers are doing that others aren't but should be. This makes it faster to coach and emulate more successful behaviors. By tracking activities by rep, leaders can also assess where coaching might have the biggest impact."

When Lauren Bailey, Founder of Factor8 and #GirlsClub and valued Outreach partner, first started in sales 20 years ago, she landed her first "big girl job" (her words) as an Inside Sales Manager. According to her, she was underqualified, overambitious, and soon underwater. And although she went through two weeks of training with her team, so were they. She wondered, "How did no one teach us how to actually do the job we were hired to do?!"

So began her quest of helping people actually feel successful at work. She's spent two decades designing new hire onboarding programs that she calls "sales rep and sales manager training that works."

But first, the payoff:

1. Revenue: She's seen between $200 K and $2 M in annual revenue returned by getting teams to quota faster.
2. Attrition: If you're losing people in the first six months, look at your training, Lauren says. She believes a good program can cut attrition in half.
3. Customer experience: You know when you get a new rep. So do your customers. You're burning leads, accounts, and future revenue.
4. Engagement: Read the studies: They're begging for better development — especially the Millennials.

Lauren knew that if she cut ramp time in half, SDRs would hit goals in about a month and a half and ISEs/AEs in about three. But not all of us have the recommended annual budget of $1,500 per rep and $3,000 per manager for development, nor do we have a Sales Training department that can actually train salespeople.

So, Lauren gave us her top 20 secrets for faster rep onboarding and ramp she learned over the past 20 years.

Secret #1: Call recordings change everything. Use a library of calls to play, pause, and discuss. Recordings get reps into the mind of the customer and teach them when to use their new skills. Hint: It's the *when to say it* that takes time and experience, not the *what*.

Secret #2: Go beyond company orientation, systems, and products and get into business and industry acumen, digital sales skills, and process (the "who and the how" to get stuff done at your company).

Secret #3: Get them obsessed with your customer base. A deep understanding of the customer situation, industry, motivators, and challenges is the secret to quick connections and faster deals.

Secret #4: Product training. Question to uncover the need, not the features and benefits of the product or service itself.

Secret #5: Get on the phones! Do it early and often. Even if it's with current customers or just for data cleansing.

Secret #6: Run systems training. This is something like timed system drills while role-playing on the phone. Integrating all the skills while selling takes reps months to master. Kick it in by the end of the first three weeks.

Secret #7: Teach managers how to call-coach and invest in a custom grading or coaching form. It's your final exam in training and aligns training with future call coaching (and seriously, managers need it).

Secret #8: Test often. Fail often. I know it took six weeks to fill the seat, but don't let them on the floor if they aren't going to make it.

Secret #9: Heavy-pour the Kool-Aid. Bury them in testimonials, calls, and stories of why customers choose you (not a quiz on company leadership and history—when should they ever use that on a call?).

Secret #10: Timing! Two days is too short, and four weeks is too long. Onboarding should focus on only their first month on the job. Bring them back for the rest. It prevents the firehose-and-forget cycle and builds confident reps ready to crush it.

Secret #11: Involve the managers. If you have a training department, I bet 50 bucks your managers don't know what's being trained. The result: Managers start over with training when reps hit the floor. An hour a week during training will save 20 teaching hours down the road. (Boom, coaching time!)

Secret #12: Managers aren't trainers. Folks, training is a profession with a right and wrong way to teach (I learned this the hard way – it's harder than you'd think). A manager in front of a class talking won't be applied or retained. Hire a trainer and then use managers to coach, test, and add color commentary.

Secret #13: Custom is king, but outsource what you can for speed. A killer program can take a year to build. Big budget holders have custom training built and licensed. Small budgets in a big hurry? Buy the training that came with your systems and outsource sales training.

Secret #14: Don't buy sales methodology—80% of a rep's time is spent trying to get that conversation. Buy sales training focused on process and phone skills. Add sexy sales methodologies like MEDDIC or SPIN Selling around level 301.

Secret #15: Try a newbie team or manager who gets all the new reps for 90 days. It frees the other leaders for big deals. And let's face it, not everyone is adept at celebrating small wins and developing people.

Secret #16: Synthesis. Never spend a whole day on systems training. Mix it up and use it together (product training + sales role-play + system entry).

Secret #17: Process. In the first six months, 75% of a rep's questions start with, "How do I …?" Teach the steps of the sale, who to go to for what, and how to find answers to a customer's top 10 questions. Try scavenger hunts and Post-It reference sheets.

Secret #18: Most e-learning sucks. Don't use it for more than 35% of your training. If you do, find microlearning, interactive modules, and multiple formats and break it up with life on the floor.

Secret #19: Call shadowing fails. Jaded reps, zoning out, bad habits—you know. Improve observation time by adding forms with what they saw and learned and what a rep could have improved.

Secret #20: Scripts = smelly fish. Messaging samples and starters are great, but never give your words to a rep and expect them to sound as good, like it, perform, or stay. Teach them to fish instead! (I might be passionate about this one!)

If you are a lucky one, you can implement 100% of these. If you're not, Lauren recommends having a line item for recruiting and tools and adding a line item for a sales trainer and an annual development budget—even if you have to reallocate a rep headcount in year one.

However, when we ask people what the hardest part about building a team is, do you know what they say? Retaining trained reps. Rep attrition is incredibly expensive and time-consuming for companies at any growth rate.

With more companies popping up and more funding being poured into companies than ever before, there are so many new job opportunities for sales reps. Between these opportunities and modern sales technology advancements, it's a great time for a career in sales!

In a highly publicized study, Glassdoor found that 68% of salespeople today are actively looking for their next job.[1] Only 19% of salespeople see themselves in their existing job for more than one year. In 2017, 26% of salespeople switched jobs. This turnover challenge is at an epidemic level. The cost and lack of productivity resulting from the turnover craze are causing global revenue inefficiency for sales teams worldwide.

Logically, this lack of sales success and efficiency is costing sales leaders their jobs. The average tenure of a VP of Sales is shrinking fast. What was a 26-month average tenure in 2010 has shrunk to only 19 months when researched in 2017 (see Figure 7.1). This lack of engagement is costing more than results to companies; it is costing leaders their jobs.

---

[1] As discussed in this blog post https://blog.hubspot.com/sales/salespeople-looking-for-new-job-infographic

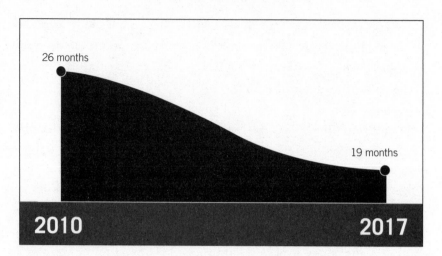

Figure 7.1 Average Length of Tenure for a Vice President of Sales

So how do you make sure you focus on not only rep effectiveness but also rep engagement from the very beginning?

HBR and CEB/Gartner have both identified that one-on-one coaching between manager and rep is the number one driver of a salesperson's intent to stay with a company. Sales leaders must make their one-on-ones with reps strategic, inspiring, and insightful in order to ignite something new in every rep on their team. The good news is reps want coaching. The better news is that if you get this meeting right, it creates an incredibly defensible competitive advantage.

For more color on one-on-one coaching, we brought in one of the most highly respected sales coaches, Rob Jeppsen. Rob was previously the SVP of Zion's Bank, where he led more than a thousand reps nationwide. Currently, he's the CEO and Founder of Xvoyant, the leading one-on-one sales rep coaching platform.

Rob's Take: The 3 Things Great Sales Leaders Do

1. **Understand the aspirations:** The most valuable thing a sales leader can know is the personal goal of each rep. What do they aspire to? Encourage your reps to challenge themselves. Aspiration creates

purpose. Purpose-driven reps conduct purpose-driven activities. If you want to drive action, add fuel to their personal fire. Understand what they aspire to and why.

Here's what great leaders do differently:

They are authentic in their desire to help reps achieve personal aspirations. To do this, you need to understand more than what an individual's aspirations are. Provide context showing how they can actually accomplish this—and more—as a member of your team. Move past the quota and into the personal goal, and action will follow.

2. **Fine-tune the transformations**: A very common statement I've heard from salespeople is: "If I knew what I needed to change in order to hit my goal, I would do it." Research shows that 90% of the time, when a rep receives what they think is coaching, they try to apply the coaching insight. Salespeople are generally willing to change if they understand why the change can help them.

   As a sales leader, the first thing you need to provide is a "well-lit pathway to success." With a good understanding of the professional aspirations of the rep, you can help them understand what activities they need to change. With Sales Engagement strategies and a tight process, you can coach based on the results of A/B tests across the team. You can also coach on insights and number of sales actions taken.

   Transformational results require transformational activities. Sales is an activity-oriented business. Either a rep needs to do more or less of something or they need to learn to do that thing better. That's where Sales Engagement can really take your coaching to the next level.

   Process is about how a salesperson uses activities to either start opportunities or advance/close opportunities. As a sales leader, use metrics to create individualized pathways to the aspirational goals of each rep. Help your reps understand the value of any activity in your process. An activity needs to do one of five things in order to be valuable:

   i. Start an opportunity
   ii. Improve revenue per customer

 iii. Improve win rate

 iv. Improve sales cycle time

 v. Advance an opportunity

Here's what great leaders do differently:

They take a paint-by-numbers approach. Start with working hard enough. If you can't explain how an activity actually matters to one of the five drivers identified above, don't track it. Your job is to create an environment where your motivated reps can win. Help create a work-back plan built on activities required to hit the aspirational goal of the rep, not your plan for them. Set activity-related goals based on the required number of activities to hit their goal. Personalized goals lead to purpose-driven engagement and interaction.

3. **Share your observations**: The one-on-one meeting is the only meeting a rep has that is 100% about them. So make sure it is about them. Once you know they're working hard enough to get them to goal given their skillset, share your observations related to their skills. This means you're listening to their calls and you're in market with them, in addition to looking at metrics. You need to be able to point to key skills that will make them do the required activities better.

Here's what great leaders do differently:

They are fair and provide clear action plans, not just feedback. To be clear, there is no substitute for your personal leadership and insight. Reps want to know that you are paying attention to them and that you personally care. Too many leaders today want to fully outsource their jobs to data. Although the data and metrics are incredibly important, don't forget that your reps still counting on *you* for inspiration and guidance too. That being said, you do need to back up your observations with data wherever possible. This will keep the conversation fair and balanced and avoid hurt feelings that a rep is being singled out or is not a favorite.

Data protects you, the leader, and gives you a common ground with the rep. SEPs easily set the table for a fair conversation by providing coaching analytics. These analytics empower both you and the rep so you can objectively view their performance, individually and compared to other team members.

Now here's where the inspirational leadership comes in: If a rep sees they are in the bottom tier, use your leadership skills to coach them rather than let them get down. They should see that this level of success *is* possible—someone else is achieving it; therefore, they can too.

SEPs make it easy to create an action plan with your reps by revealing best practices like sequence blueprints, the best time of day to contact a certain persona, and much more. With this combination of data and your personal leadership, even a low-performing rep should walk out of their one-on-one meeting whistling.

When someone joins your team, they are giving you cycles in their professional career. As leaders, you owe it to them to help them be wildly successful. If you do this right, they will stay with you for a very long time.

Chapter 8

Account-based Sales Strategies for the Modern Seller

Most companies embracing modern Sales Engagement are focused on contacting accounts with multiple stakeholders and decision makers. This happens as companies go "up market" and sell to bigger and bigger companies. Although the general approach has been around for decades, the modernization of Account-based Sales and Account-based Marketing is paving a new path for salespeople everywhere.

Defining an Account-based Approach

Account-based is the coordination of highly valuable, personalized experiences across all functions that impact a customer (marketing, sales development, sales, and customer success) to drive engagement at a target set of accounts. In this world, sales enjoys better opportunities but fewer of them. Account-based is about building relationships at target accounts deemed the right company, regardless of whether there is an active buying process. To be successful, every engagement is customized to the account and tailored to the individual stakeholder. In this new model, successful sales reps have a SWAT team of execution partners from Sales Development, Marketing, executive staff, and internal experts.

To help cover the bases (pun intended) of Account-based Sales, we brought in our friend Dan Gottlieb, Lead Analyst for Account-based Sales at TOPO Inc. TOPO is one of the leading analyst firms focused on helping high-growth companies build Account-based Sales and Marketing strategies. They work with hundreds of top venture-backed and the fastest-growing companies, such as Twilio, Netsuite, Outreach, Procore, ServiceNow, and many more.

According to Dan, there are five key characteristics that define an Account-based Sales strategy:

1. **Targeted, high-value accounts**: All companies targeted and engaged in this model fit or closely resemble the ICP. This transforms a list of accounts to penetrate into a canonical target account list worthy of the organization dedicating time and money toward converting.

2. **Data- and intelligence-driven programs and campaigns**: High-quality data and intelligence are essential to account-based success. By pinpointing account-level attributes and accurate contact data, marketing and sales can more effectively engage buyers at these accounts.

3. **Cross-functional orchestration**: Sequenced coordination of different activities, programs, and campaigns across marketing, sales development, sales, and customer success helps drive engagement with multiple stakeholders in target accounts.

4. **Valuable and personalized experiences**: Account-based sales requires companies to deliver relevant and personalized high-value offers, or sales plays, to specific buyers.

5. **Coordinated, high-frequency, high-effort outreach**: Account-based requires continuous high-touch, high-frequency campaigns against the target account list. Instead of focusing on measuring

activities or activities in bulk, account-based organizations plan and track activities by target account.

Account-based Plays Are Key to Converting Target Accounts

Dan believes that any account-based strategy needs to manifest itself in a set of tactics that marketing and sales can use to engage target accounts—he calls these tactics "plays." The most successful account-based programs leverage plays that engage buyers with valuable experiences and convert at a higher rate than traditional marketing tactics.

The idea behind high-value offers is to present prospects with an offer so valuable that they need to engage with the offer via a seller. These offers are typically focused on a high-priority challenge confronting or an opportunity available to the target account (or segment of target accounts). Moreover, they are often personalized to the target account, providing prescriptive insights and best practices to the buyer. They do not replace fundamental account-selling methodologies (like discovery calls) but instead enhance a solid sales process.

Account-based Sales plays directly align to the sales process and can be broken into four categories:

1. **High-value first meeting**: Goal is to capture enough interest to encourage a meeting. Examples include:
   a. **Custom content plays**: SDRs for a Software-as-a-Service (SaaS) company research and create a custom report using a template developed by Marketing.
   b. **Vertical content plays**: Marketing develops a report focused on a particular drug segment (e.g., diabetes) for pharma companies, presented by an internal expert.
   c. **Use case plays**: Leverage a compelling use case to schedule a meeting to tell a relevant business transformation story.

2. **Post discovery**: Goal is to use the insights gathered during the first meeting to personalize content with the goal of engaging stakeholders early and inviting additional stakeholders into the process. These plays rely on effective and proper discovery. Examples include:

    a. **Semi-custom, high-value content**: Insert three to five insights collected in discovery into a "readiness assessment" template; present to create urgency.

    b. **On-site workshops**: IT security vendors deliver free security audits in an onsite workshop; map the prospect's current experience and identify gaps.

    c. **Tailored campaigns to additional stakeholders**: Leverage intelligence from discovery to launch a multitouch campaign to additional stakeholders.

3. **Customized sales**: These are what a seller does to tailor every interaction with a prospect and, ultimately, what captures the behaviors of high-performing sellers. The following plays should be customized for every buyer in an Account-based Sales process:

    a. **Presentations**: Marketing creates the deck and the main content but provides templates for sales reps to articulate the account's current challenges and initiatives; use the 80/20 rule to execute at scale.

    b. **Demos**: Highly customized demo, including a prospect's real data, business process, and, when applicable, logo.

    c. **Champion content**: Customizable PDFs for sales reps to share with stakeholders based on account and disposition; sales reps pick and choose relevant content, lightly customize it for the prospect, bundle, and send.

4. **Close**: The goal of these plays is for marketing to support sales by enabling sellers to deliver a high-value, customized sales process at the close stage. Examples include:

    a. **Deal brochures**: Beautifully designed, lightly customized, printed deal brochure to accompany the proposal and address customers' key challenges and the proposed solution.

b. **Close plans**: A timeline of key milestones already achieved and milestones going forward through implementation kickoff.

c. **Late-stage marketing**: A sales team targeting Sales Ops and sales leaders sends bagels and coffee to the prospects' end-of-quarter sales meetings.

Effective SDR Marketing Orchestration Is Critical to Execute High-value Offers

TOPO research shows organizations that have met or exceeded their expectations within a year of implementing account-based share one common trait: effective orchestration in Account-based Sales Development.

The fastest path to launching orchestrated campaigns that deliver strong results is to focus on marketing–sales development orchestration. SDR marketing-coordinated campaigns produce lift in target account pipeline. Organizations running these plays typically realize a 30% to 50% lift in meetings set at target accounts, with some organizations reporting a 100% increase.[1]

Sales Engagement Technology Is Critical for Account-based Sales Play Execution

One of the most crucial touches in account-based is SDR and sales outreach—this is executed at scale via Sales Engagement technology. Sales Engagement technology enables sales departments to efficiently deliver high-quality interactions with prospects and customers at scale. In effective account-based programs, multiple touches are delivered via multiple channels and these touches are delivered, tracked, and managed via technology. For example, direct mail, which is traditionally viewed as a manual exercise, can now be delivered via direct mail automation.

---

[1] Captured via TOPO account-based research interviews (2016–2017) and discussed at: https://blog.topohq.com/achieving-account-based-orchestration-via-marketing-sdr-collaboration/

The platform that manages these interactions is the SEP, a critical component of the SDR marketing orchestration machine. The SEP is a single interface to efficiently plan, execute, track, measure, and optimize interactions between sales and target accounts across multiple touches and channels. As a segment, TOPO research shows that SEPs have seen the fastest growth of all technologies in the overall Sales Engagement category: 92% of Sales Development organizations rank SEPs as critical to their team's success, and 90% of sales leaders plan to invest in technologies/methodologies to help their sellers engage effectively with prospects and customers.[2]

An important factor driving the growth of the Sales Engagement market is that quota-carrying reps are starting to adopt engagement tools to streamline mid- and late-stage sales plays. In the future, engagement will expand beyond sales and SDRs to all customer-facing departments. For example, optimizing the customer success or customer marketing process using similar or identical sales plays will become a strategic imperative for organizations. An SEP's capacity to facilitate multichannel orchestration and execution from a single platform will turn Account Managers into Customer Marketers.

In addition to core functionality, conversational intelligence and the emergence of next best actions will offer an unprecedented level of insight into the needs of buyers at target accounts. Moreover, these capabilities will surface the proper high-value offer sales plays an account-based team should run based on the needs of the buyer.

We have seen phenomenal insights.

Dan raises great points. When looking into our own data from our sales team here at Outreach, we can see that in many instances, we have more than 20 different contacts at one company, all of whom are important to getting the deal done. This is a major reason why having an account-based approach is so important to winning these bigger deals. And not

---

[2] TOPO 2016 Sales Development Benchmark Report and TOPO 2017 Sales Development Technology Benchmark Report, discussed at: https://blog.topohq.com/sales-engagement-the-definitive-guide/

just winning them but also expanding and upselling them even after they've been won! More and more stakeholders are introduced, especially if you have multiple product lines that span new functions across the organization. We have a saying around here that goes, "Winning is just the beginning!" This is more commonly known as "Land and Expand."

Twenty or more is an extreme case, but even the smaller deals have multiple stakeholders that need to be nurtured and reengaged frequently.

Julianne's Take: My Journey into Account-Based Sales

I was tasked with setting in-person meetings with Directors/VPs of IT and CIOs for enterprise companies. This was 'back in the day' before Sales Engagement Platforms existed, so we were working on spreadsheets and sticky notes to remember when to follow up with a prospect. We were delivering the same pitch on every cold call, handling objections the same ways every time, etc.

Then I started reading about Account-based Sales. Research from CEB shows us that there are 6.8 decision makers involved in a B2B purchasing decision. Why on earth was I only reaching out to one? Rather than calling a single decision maker at one company and then moving onto the next, I changed my strategy to focus on the companies I target.

What are the components of some of our most successful customers? How can I access the data to help me define those characteristics in prospective customers? Cold calls became much warmer. Researching the account became much more critical. Understanding how to communicate with different personas was key. Smiling and dialing wasn't the name of the game anymore; we shifted to a world of better understanding our prospects' situations, the challenges they encounter, and positioning our solution in a way that they understood exactly how we solve them.

Let's go back to the 6.8 decision makers. Later in the sales cycle, deals typically involve sign-offs from Finance, Legal, and in some situations HR or IT—but let's put those aside and focus on three target profiles we should start with.

- End user: These are tactical players who care about the details because they will use the product or service day in and day out. This will make them perform better and, in turn, look good.
- Management/leadership: They usually want to know how you can save them time or make them money. This will make their overall numbers better, making them look good.
- Economic buyer: Forces management, pulls funds from other areas, and creates a budget for your product or service. This will make the team more efficient, thus making them—you guessed it—look good too!

In most situations, salespeople sell to positions that they have never been in. So how do we know what's important to them?

Ask them questions and interview your customers. What impact does your solution provide? Why did you purchase this solution? Questions that will uncover how others in their roles might also be considering a technology purchase of similar size or of a similar situation.

Thanks, Julianne! By the way, this is another way to think about the persona exercises introduced in Chapter 3.

Now, you might be at this point in the book and say to yourself, "But at the end of the day, sales is all about relationships, right?"

In the next section, Jonathan Mayer, SDR Manager from $15 billion dollar company Splunk, explains why the answer to this question is "yes"—but not in the way you might think.

Jonathan's Take: The Sales Relationship That Really Matters

You've probably heard that line from every veteran salesperson you've ever met—and maybe you've used it yourself to explain how you took down your first big account. But if you listen a little closer, the top sales reps will let you in on the best-kept secret in account-based selling: Many times, the relationships that matter aren't the ones you have with your buyers; they're the ones your buyers have with each other.

In order to take down the tough deals, or to land the territory-building accounts, you need to activate a buying team inside your account that will sell your deal even when you're not there. Your deal needs to become *their* deal—and buyers generally are terrible sellers. Account-based selling starts with spending some time figuring out who's on your internal selling team (and who's not) and then teaching them how to sell.

If you've spent any time in a sales training class in the past 20 years, you've heard about buyer roles—champions, coaches, influencers, blockers, technical evaluators—and you've probably used them in your forecast calls to show off how well you know your accounts.

We're not going to recreate those ideas in detail here—they're well covered in modern sales methodologies.

Instead, I'll ask you to consider how the buyers in your account are oriented to change—and what that means for them personally.

If you don't have a business problem to solve, there's no reason for your account to buy your solution. But beyond business change, how will adopting your solution change the role of your buyers within their organization? Are they gaining responsibility or control they didn't have before, and is that a personal win for them? If the change is a welcome one, you have a potential seller. If not, you have a blocker.

To get them selling, consider how your solution fits into their personal value proposition. This is the reason they were hired, or perhaps the reason they survived the last round of layoffs. If their boss called them into the conference room and said, "I'm firing someone today. Tell me why it shouldn't be you," their personal value proposition would be the first words out of their mouth.

Perhaps they are the technical expert—their value to the business is knowing exactly how everything works. Hopefully, you've shown them how your solution is going to fix all the things they know are broken. Give them the details they need to solidify their position as the expert and insider access to your own technical resources. Make sure they have opportunities to demonstrate that expertise at important milestones in the project, and coach them through how to summarize the technical improvements to nontechnical team members. When you're not there, this seller is sharing insight into what they've learned by seeing the problem the way your company sees the problem, using your language to define it. When you show up to speak with other team members, you'll sound just like the technical expert they already trust.

If the change is not a welcome one for someone on the buying team, you'll need to consider the second question: How much influence does each buyer have? Hopefully, your blockers have low influence. These blockers are easy to spot—they are resistant to change because they've been pushed to the edge of the power base and they're afraid of becoming irrelevant. Low-influence blockers usually own the status quo. You're already well on your way to neutralizing them by equipping your sellers with personal value propositions for your solution, isolating your blockers even further from what they want: more influence.

But high-influence blockers are a different story. If they want change, but not *your* change, you have a competitor's champion (more on them shortly). If they don't want change at all, you'll need your own champion—who has more influence than they do—to do some major selling on your behalf. The biggest challenge is figuring out who that is—and that's why you need a coach.

Coaches give you the low-down on who's who in the account. They are not only willing to meet with you and share business priorities and operational details, but they also understand the political structure of the buying team or power base. When old guard sales reps say, "Selling is all about relationships," this is the relationship they are talking about. This person *likes* you. If you suspect you have a competitor's champion in play, pull out the corporate card and start hosting happy hours because you need a friend on the inside who will stay late and give you the whole story. Don't forget to trust but validate what you hear from coaches. Their intentions may be good though their facts may be wrong.

Eventually, your coach is going to lead you to a potential champion. You'll know you're there when you find a high-influence, change-welcoming buyer who will personally benefit by making your solution their solution to a business problem they own. Because this is your chief seller when you're not there, you'll want to make sure you've positioned them for success.

Start by validating their influence. At some point, your champion is going to need to put you in front of the decision maker and say, "This is the guy who is going to solve our problem." A true champion is so close to the decision maker that they are nearly peers, so a meeting shouldn't be a problem—ask for one. If it is, they aren't truly in the power base. You might still be able to get your deal done, but more often than not, it's going to "slip" when a higher priority comes along from someone with more influence (remember that competitor's champion?).

The next step is to build your solution into a personal win for your champion.

Their personal value proposition is probably ownership of an important piece of the business, so you need to understand how your solution is going to affect the business relationship they have with the decision maker, as well as all the other buyers you've been turning into sellers along the way.

But good news! Your champion demonstrates their value to the decision maker by showing up with a solution that already has momentum and buy-in, which good decision makers know are keys to mitigating the risk of failure. If you've done your job right, you've activated a network of goal-aligned sellers that your champion (and you) can use again and again to get things done. That is an extremely appealing asset for a decision maker, a great personal win for your champion, and ultimately what Account-based Selling is all about.

If you've ever wondered how the "big accounts" salespeople get that job, this is how: In their interviews, they walk through how they built a network of sellers for a high-influence champion in a major account, and they usually have done it in such a way that the same network can be reactivated on a whole new solution. That's how you get entrusted with a big league quota and spend every April at President's Club.

Jonathan summed this up perfectly, but it doesn't stop there.

Eliminate the Dreaded Handoff

Ensuring that the right post-sales process takes place actually begins at the beginning of the sale. If you're treating the handoff of customer information from sales to client services as a fixed event, you're not creating the best buyer experience for the new client. With account-based selling, Customer Success Managers (CSMs) should be stepping in earlier in the sales process, and the handoff should be a natural process for the customer and the supplier.

Outreach customer Blake Harber, Director of Sales at the rapidly growing Lucidchart, recommends ensuring all critical information your reps use is automatically and seamlessly available to the post-sales teams, which includes more than just Salesforce notes. Build a system so that the critical information and key relationships that were discovered early in the sales cycle are available and accessible for all post-sales teams, without a sales rep sharing it manually (because that usually doesn't happen). If this type of information doesn't make its way to CSMs, the implementation team ends up doing the discovery process all over again with a new customer. This obviously creates a bad customer experience, and it can impact the future relationship with the account.

And with recent studies showing that as much as 75% of your revenue can come after the initial sale, this negative experience can significantly reduce the opportunities for cross-selling, upselling, and even renewal. All the more reason to treat the account holistically and incentivize sales reps to take ownership of an account through the entire sales process.

Account-based Sales is more than just account organization, proven plays, mapping profiles and personas, and getting the deal across the finish line. It's about making them all talk to each other, even beyond closing the sale. It's about empowering your relationships to build better relationships with their peers. It's about carrying those relationships through the renewals. This is where true alignment begins.

If it were easy, everyone would be closing big deals. However, with modern Sales Engagement, it's becoming more process-driven, repeatable, and replicable than ever before—and that's a great thing for sellers everywhere.

Chapter 9

How to Align Modern Sales, Success, and Marketing with Sales Engagement

S ales, Marketing, and Customer Success alignment is a crucial element of any functional Sales Engagement strategy. Without it, the three orgs that make up your revenue team are essentially lost. They're on different pages. They *must* share feedback from the front lines, from customers, and share what messaging is resonating. This is the only way for a revenue organization to be fully prepared to sell and market in the modern era of fast-paced revenue generation.

Jen Spencer talked about developing personas with marketing to master your outreach in Chapter 3. Julianne Thompson told us how important it was to speak to your customers and understand why they bought and how the solution is helping them in Chapter 8. Now it's time to take modern revenue alignment to the next level, starting with Sales and Marketing alignment first.

All good revenue teams have the same things in common. They're aligned on many of these key elements.

13 Elements of a Successful Cross-org Alignment Strategy

- **Kill the MQL**. Teams need mutually agreed upon metrics to track success.

- **Agree on a reliable attribution model**. Metrics are all well and good but not if you can't track the source they're coming from. Attribution is key.

- **Possess an integrated tech stack**. CRM, Marketing Automation, and Sales Engagement is a common starting point, but then add other tech layers as needed and ensure the whole ecosystem seamlessly integrates.

- **Agree on an inclusive event strategy**. Know the right events, the right people to send to, and the right tracks to speak on per audience.

- **Create an aligned messaging strategy**. Be clear on the holistic message *and* who is the key messenger for each facet—a thought leadership matrix can work wonders here.

- **Keep a steady communication cadence**. Modern Sales and Marketing departments move at light speed. Are you meeting daily, twice a week, once a week, or less? If less, you might not be very well-aligned.

- **Orchestrate a proper handoff**. This is also known as the Service Level Agreement (SLA) between different orgs.

- **Maintain quality, clean, centralized data**. Accessible and functional data is key.

- **Attend regular customer offsites**. Hear what customers really think by getting out of the office together. Doing it with your revenue counterpart can provide you answers to questions you may not have asked but you may find super valuable.

- **Loop in Customer Success**. We hear a lot about Sales and Marketing alignment, but Customer Success is no longer just a nice to add. It's a *must* add.

- **Build personas**. We talked a lot about them because they're key to aligning the company around how to speak to different cohorts of customers and potential customers.

- **Cultivate a deep understanding of the buyer's journey**. Familiarize your teams with what your buyer behavior is from high-funnel buying signals to the moment they renew.
- **Exhibit empathy**. This one goes without saying. At the end of the day, you're a team. Have each other's backs.

To keep our content coming directly from the doers who know the ins and outs, we brought in our Marketing Campaigns extraordinaire Lauren Alt to give us some insider tips. Let's dive right into the first two.

Kill the MQL

"The first rule of alignment," says Lauren, "is never say 'Marketing Qualified Leads (MQL). This is a rule the Outreach Demand Gen team preaches wherever we go. It's amazing how varied the response is. If you say it to a room full of sales leaders, you'll get a standing ovation. Say it in a marketing context, however, and you may be ducking rotten tomatoes. How can two revenue orgs be so far apart?"

As Lauren explains it, the MQL has been a standard way for marketers to qualify and prioritize leads for sales organizations for many years. "There's still value in creating a standardized, repeatable way of passing marketing leads to sales," she notes, "but its meaning is defined differently at each organization, therefore diminishing its value and causing confusion. At Outreach, we still use MQL as a predictive indicator of success. But we no longer use it as a metric of success. MQLs are not a vanity metric because without the top of the funnel, you don't have a bottom of the funnel. But it's a means to an end, not an end in itself."

"There is one metric that all business leaders alike can speak to: money."

—Lauren Alt, Campaigns Manager at Outreach

"When Marketing leaders find their 'joint North Star' with their Sales counterparts and start reporting on contributed pipeline and overall revenue lift, that's when you will be able to speak the same language," Lauren says. "If you want to make this easier, make sure to invest in Sales and Marketing Engagement technology that gives you access to these critical low-funnel metrics."

Developing a Reliable Attribution Model

Lauren's second tip expands on the importance of attribution. "It's easy to say marketers should speak the same language as their sales counterpart, but it's another to actually do it," she says. "Developing a reliable attribution model that is representative of true revenue lift is one of the most difficult things to do when building your strategy, but it's absolutely critical to achieving Sales and Marketing alignment.

"Successful marketers use data to make business decisions when it comes to driving growth," she adds. "Being able to back Marketing's priorities up with data helps build a bridge with Sales leaders who can often feel disconnected to marketing objectives."

Attribution cannot be limited to a static moment in time but rather must reflect a cohesive buyer's journey. This is why traditional "first-touch" or "last-touch" models no longer cut it, Lauren says. She recommends using a multitouchpoint attribution model, like Bizible, to help see the full picture of how Marketing is influencing their Sales team's deals.

Thanks for the awesome tips, Lauren! Next up, let's talk tech.

Find the Right Bridge Technology

For many organizations, the chasm between Sales and Marketing isn't philosophical; it's functional. Most orgs still do not run on a single platform that allows Sales and Marketing to have joint global visibility into data and activity. Instead, companies experience the age-old stalemate where Sales eats, sleeps, and breathes CRM while Marketing swears by their Marketing Automation platform. Sound familiar?

Without the right bridge technology, there will be too much friction to facilitate alignment, no matter how muchgood will there is between the two departments. The good news is there is new emerging technology that allows orgs to centralize visibility for the first time. Investing in such a technology is an indispensable step in alignment.

This is where SEPs really help align all revenue teams. Your entire Sales, Marketing, and even Customer Success teams can live in one place that connects seamlessly to your data, account info, approved messaging, collateral, and other applications—without a break in the chain.

Expand Your Event Horizons

This is another area where all functions within the revenue team can help each other massively. Sales and Success can help Marketing understand which events to select based on attendee profiles. They can also help with content and talk tracks for speaking sessions based on what current customers care about at the moment. At Outreach, when GDPR came out, we leveraged the hype around it to add it to all of our talk tracks at events. This was a big way in which our frontline Sales and Success people were able to influence Marketing-led campaigns.

We're big believers in getting Sales and Marketing and Sales and Success leaders in the same room. When planning your next industry event, it pays to double your guest list—even if you have to up the champagne budget a little. Today, it pays to have Sales events that include Marketers or Sales events that include Customer Success, regardless of the vertical you're in.

Events are ground zero for learning new best practices, getting educated on new products in the market, and, of course, networking over a friendly drink or bite after the show. The more your revenue teams engage in these activities together, the more aligned they will naturally become. These events are great opportunities for cross-department alignment.

Max's Take: Align on a Messaging Strategy

Misalignment between Sales and Marketing can be incredibly destructive to the success of both individual initiatives and companywide efforts. There are many types of misalignment issues. One of the main ones? Messaging.

When I think about misalignment between departments, a few prime examples come to mind.

One of these stories happened to me personally, and one is a more well-known industry example. The background on the more well-known example is that a salesperson (or more likely a marketing engine) sent a very ill-informed e-mail to Werner Vogels, Chief Technology Officer of Amazon, asking him about his migration to the cloud. The e-mail opened with a question: "Is your company still considering going to the cloud?" For those of you who don't know, Werner pretty much invented the cloud at Amazon. Needless to say, Werner couldn't resist taking a screenshot of the e-mail and sharing it on Twitter, saying, "I know your targeting algorithm was cheap and thus not perfect, but I suggest you ask for your money back from whomever sold it to you!" Ouch.

Something similar happened to our friend and partner John Barrows. John has an incredible sales messaging program under his firm, JBarrows Training.

John recalls a time when a sales rep sent him one of those typical e-mail sequences with a bunch of templated e-mails focused on how great their company and product suite was. John told us, "The sequence included the expected 'guilt e-mail' and ultimately the 'breakup e-mail.' I don't usually pay much attention to these e-mails, but on this particular day, for whatever reason, I decided to let the rep know how I felt.

"Straight to the point, I said something along the lines of, 'The reason I'm not responding is that I'm tired of receiving these templated e-mails; they're doing more harm than good, and I'm sick of sales reps going through the motions without thinking about what they are sending!' The poor rep … but he had it coming. The rep later wrote he understood my frustration and also pointed out that he wasn't the one who sent the e-mails – his Marketing department did."

John firmly believes that Marketing should market and Sales should sell. When Marketing tries to pretend they are Sales, they do way more harm than good. Marketing writes e-mails that sound like they're coming from Sales, but the reader usually knows, often in seconds, that these e-mails are far from personally customized. As soon as your recipient figures out that the messages they're receiving are automated (or developed by a robot in the case of artificial intelligence [AI]), they stop trusting that rep entirely and begin deleting every single e-mail from that brand. Without aligning the roles of Sales and Marketing, you're actively contributing to the growth of distrust in your target audience.

John believes that the solution to this misalignment is related to a concept he says he borrowed from Gary Vaynerchuk: "If content is king, then context is god."[1] He relates this to marketing versus sales: Marketing is content; sales is context.

"If we as sales professionals are not putting any context around our content, then we're no different from Marketing, and I have no idea why we're getting paid to do what we do," John said. Sending out template e-mails, making generic cold calls with a script, pressing play on demos— this is all content. Sales reps aren't needed for any of that these days. They need to take the content that Marketing is developing and make it relevant and personalized to the individual they are communicating with. Without this context, the misalignment between Sales and Marketing will just continue to get worse, and sales reps will become less and less relevant."

Well said, John. Leveraging an SEP can create a major advantage here.

[1] https://www.garyvaynerchuk.com/content-is-king-but-context-is-god/

Max's Take: Constant Cross-team Communication

A few weeks ago, I attended an event that one of our investors put together. The main talk track of the day was a session between Sanjay Dholakia and Bill Binch. They were the Chief Marketing Officer and Chief Revenue Officer of Marketo as it rose from nothing to a company that had an initial public offering (IPO) of more than a billion dollars.

They told a story of how, when they first met, they knew it was so important to be aligned that they would have dinner and drinks together every Monday night at the same restaurant and force themselves to get closer. This led to a deeper bond that would undoubtedly translate to the workplace. Now, I'm not evangelizing getting wasted with your Marketing counterpart to start each week, but what I am asking is this: Are you doing the things you need to do to really align with Marketing?

At Outreach, our Head of Marketing and our Head of Sales are on anywhere between three and five calls or meetings per week together. Same with our Head of Customer Success. They speak almost daily. In order to be fully aligned, come up with a rhythm of calls or meetings that allows you to clear any roadblocks, review metrics, learn anything new coming out of that org, or just make them feel heard.

A Proper Handoff

If not properly done, this can be the leaky bucket syndrome of modern revenue orgs. There are few things more important than a proper hand-off because not having one almost nullifies the rest of the work that's been done. A poor Marketing-to-Sales handoff can kill a closable deal in its tracks. A poor Sales-to-Success handoff can botch a closed deal and start things off on a rocky footing, hampering your odds for renewal.

In many orgs, this is called a Service Level Agreement or SLA. It is a defined contract that both the one providing the handoff and the one receiving the handoff sign, signifying that the buyer is qualified and the handoff was made properly. This way, there is no fighting later because the revenue org leaders can point back to the document being signed by both sides.

Clean, Centralized Data

We're not going to write too much about this one as it goes without saying, but it would be an incredible handicap to try to run a team that doesn't have clean, accessible, and organized data. If this is an issue for your org, you may want to start your alignment process here.

Get Out and Visit Customers

Our frontline Sales and Success teams are always on the road visiting customers and prospects. But what about Marketing? We send a few of our product marketers on the road at least once per month to visit four or five customers at a time. We do lunch and learns, where we set up time to buy them lunch and bring it to their office and then sit down with them for an hour and talk about Outreach and Sales Engagement. It helps us speak the same language as the customer and our customer-facing teams and even empower our customer-facing teams better than before.

Including Customer Success in Your Sales and Marketing Alignment Is No Longer a Maybe but a *Must*

For the following section, we tapped a partner of ours, Todd Eby of the firm SuccessHACKER. SuccessHACKER is the premier customer success training and consulting firms that works with many of the customer success orgs at the world's fastest-growing companies. Here, he breaks down how to think about Customer Success when it comes to aligning with Sales and Marketing.

Todd's Take: They're Not Buying A Drill-bit; They're Buying A Hole

Unless your current ideal buying persona looks like anyone with a pulse, a wallet, and a willingness to spend their money with you, then you need to know what their desired outcome is.

To do this, you need to focus on understanding your buyers, getting very clear on what success looks like to them and how you'll deliver. How do you do that?

Ultimately, it comes down to knowing the Jobs-To-Be-Done (JTBD) for each persona.

Once you know the jobs the buyer wants to get done—why they want to "hire" your solution—it enables you to deepen the level of engagement because you're able to speak to how you're going to help them achieve their goals and solve their challenges.

Jobs-To-Be-Done

Created by Tony Ulwick and popularized by Harvard Business School Professor Clayton Christensen in his book, *The Innovator's Solution,*[2] Jobs-To-Be-Done is an approach that enables companies to understand the job the customer is trying to execute when they are using a product or offering.

The JTBD process enables companies to break down their customers' "job-to-be-done" into discrete jobs that can then be easily mapped back to the delivery of the customers' desired outcomes.

Capturing Buyer Jobs

To get started, you need to identify what the buyer's main JTBD are. These are what I refer to as the buyer's "super" jobs. These are the critical jobs that your customers "hire" your product for.

---

[2] https://www.amazon.com/Innovators-Solution-Creating-Sustaining-Successful/dp/1422196577

Some personas may already include this information in varying formats and level of detail. Typically, it's captured in the needs, goals, and challenges sections of the standard persona. The challenge is that there's little detail beyond "generate more leads" or "increase our conversions."

How do you get started with enriching this information? First, let's start with understanding what a job is. A job describes the task a customer is trying to execute; it's why customers buy products, services, and solutions.

There are two different types of JTBDs:

1. Main Jobs-To-Be-Done: Describes the critical task that the customers want to achieve
2. Related Jobs-To-Be-Done: What customers want to do in conjunction with the main jobs

To capture both types of jobs, I recommend using the following job statements formula:

Action Verb + Object of the Action + Clarification of the Context

Example: Capture prospect e-mail addresses when they download our content so that we can capture them as a lead.

Getting started with capturing your buyer's jobs:

1. Start by capturing all the things that your customers do with your product as job statements. To begin, go back to your five to 10 most successful customers and determine what they were trying to accomplish and how they're using your product to do it. Document the features that they're using and what they're using them to do.
2. Organize this information into a hierarchy that provides you with a list of features and use cases that is categorized.
3. Convert this information into job statements. Make sure to categorize the jobs. Look for the jobs that are parents of the other jobs and organize accordingly.

4. Organize the jobs by the order in which they need to occur. Focus on the first-order jobs—these are the "must get done" jobs for your customers to reach initial value. Organize the remaining by looking at value and the traction/stickiness they deliver. You want to use your model customers to determine which jobs represent your most common path to first value and beyond.

Using JTBD to understand all the jobs that your customer could "hire" you for will enable you to enrich your current personas to the point that they work not only for Sales and Marketing but also for Customer Success.

The new, enriched personas will provide you with a common understanding of your customers and enable a common language to form around the buyer.

The expanded set will also ensure that you're not solely selling to the buyer's needs. They'll ensure that you are also addressing the influencers and end users who are the ones who will be working to deliver the buyer's desired outcome (as well as their own).

Although Todd's strategy is a solid one, we want to go deeper on aligning around personas because they're just so incredibly important to a strong Sales Engagement process.

Sales, Marketing, and Customer Success Alignment in Persona-based Research

If Marketing owns the development of buyer personas in your organization (which is recommended), it's imperative that the Sales and Customer Success teams are involved in validating the persona research. After all, it is both sales and customer success reps who are on the front lines interacting with current and future customers on a daily basis. Involving these teams will also help Marketing secure necessary buy-in to ensure the persona research is used and doesn't end up languishing in the Marketing department.

Once cross-org alignment is in place, you can operationalize this alignment pact by leveraging technology to build personas into your salesperson's workflow. How, you ask? You can include persona details right in your SEP and then the information will be available right there within the salesperson's communication activities. This is just one way SEPs remove friction from the busy salesperson's daily job.

Pro Tips for Practical Application of Personas in the Sales Process

Once you've built your personas and incorporated feedback from Sales and Customer Success, the real fun begins! Personas are powerful—now you can truly enable your team to better serve your customers while helping them close more business—a win for everyone.

Jen Spencer, VP of Sales and Marketing at SmartBug Media, spills her secrets for creating personas salespeople will actually use. "Marketers should enable their Sales teams with bite-sized buyer persona overviews, or battle cards, that help sales reps understand the best ways to communicate with these individuals," Jen recommends. According to Jen, if your buyer persona documentation for Hannah is a four-slide-long documentary, how can you reduce it to just a trailer of the most relevant tidbits? Jen recommends that marketers whittle their personas down by internal audience. "Marketers should organize these battlecards by which information is most relevant to our SDR, which information makes the most sense for the Demand Gen team, and so on," Jen says.

In addition, if your Sales team has SDRs who are reaching out to prospects

> *"While everyone in the company should have access and be encouraged to read the complete buyer persona research, a quick overview is helpful for new team members in particular to review prior to engaging with a buyer."*
>
> *—Jen Spencer, VP of Sales and Marketing at SmartBug Media*

who have engaged with content offers on your website, Marketing should take advantage of the opportunity to enable reps with persona-based talking points for each content offer.

"It's overly optimistic to assume your Sales team will read every piece of content created by Marketing, let alone be prepared to speak to the appropriate messaging for each persona," says Jen. "Trust me. I learned this the hard way." Instead, she suggests a simple, one-page overview for each campaign is sufficient to enable your Sales team to meet the needs of your future customers.

On the operations side, Sales teams should utilize their martech stack to segment lists of contacts based on personas, Jen recommends: "For example, rather than jumping around from one contact to another at random, it's more efficient for a sales rep to carve out time to focus on interactions by persona. This helps keep psychographic details fresh and allows for more consistent communications."

Jen also recommends that Marketing and Sales work collaboratively to identify trends in the digital footprint of each persona and even build out internal notifications based on persona-specific interactions. "For example, you might discover that a member of the buying committee is likely to visit your API documentation page during a particular stage in the sales process," says Jen. "A triggered notification could alert the sales rep that the opportunity appears to have progressed internally and a technical conversation with an extended audience needs to be scheduled. Or, seeing a Marketing Qualified Lead actively engaging on the pricing page might be an excellent time to pick up the phone and engage with that individual while they are exhibiting a qualification signal."

Awesome tips, Jen!

Once you've aligned Sales and Marketing around persona research and your Sales team is actively using this research to support their efforts, you'll undoubtedly discover many other practical applications that make sense in your organization. The key to continued success is increased communication and open sharing of what's working and what's not while always keeping your customers at the center of your efforts.

Understanding the Buyer's Journey

Finally, all of that persona work is paying off! Now that you're aligned across Sales, Marketing, and Customer Success, it's time to piece together the customer journey map. This is a map outline of all the touchpoints and interactions a buyer has with your company over the course of their full lifetime experience with your brand.

Typically, a customer journey map details every step of the buying and renewal process, the exact touchpoints, the feeling or emotion you want them to receive from the messaging at that point, along with the revenue org and exact individuals responsible for working with the customer at that place in the journey.

These living maps can help you optimize your process by removing friction or barriers to entry, properly place the right content with the right context at the right time, and potentially make customer acquisition and renewal more efficient from a financial standpoint.

A great site resource for this is designingcx.com.

Last But Not Least: Establishing Empathy

Sometimes when you're hyperfocused on the data, you can lose focus on the human element that is the backbone of a successful sales and marketing strategy. Looking at deals and pipeline as strictly an object in your CRM can create a narrowed mindset when trying to think big picture. To have true alignment between revenue leaders, you need to start with the basic human element of empathy.

Empathy is often used to discuss the foundation of customer and prospect relationships, but your internal counterpart can sometimes be the hardest to empathize with. The easiest way to establish empathy across teams is to increase communication around one another's priorities, goals, and objectives. Once you start understanding your counterpart's daily struggles, you'll likely understand their role is critical to you finding success.

3

Future Proofing: Where Sales Engagement Fits and What's Next

Chapter 10

Building a Modern Sales Tech Stack

Technology is accelerating at an unprecedented pace. In the past five years, sales technology vendors multiplied from being in the dozens to the low thousands. CRM is no longer enough.

Yes, buyers have more options than ever before and more information at their fingertips, but salespeople now have more weapons in their arsenal. These new technologies are leveraging machine learning and natural language processing to do everything from sentiment analysis to e-mail responses, relaying buying signals and intent data, analyzing phone calls for phrases and details to say or not say that help close deals or kill them, and much more.

A good CRM can take you a long way, but at some point, you are going to want to do more than capture data and move through opportunity stages.

When it's time to build your tech stack, your design and approach are critical to success, both in driving adoption and creating a balanced ecosystem of tools. The goal is removing friction from the sales process without overcomplicating the behavioral expectations of the sales team.

A new tech stack should be like a puzzle with each piece creating a clearer view of how the sales process leads to closing more deals. The right design and foundation are crucial for future success. A great designer considers the long game, creating a layered ecosystem of tools that can support the wide variety of sales and marketing strategies that could happen over time.

To help us go deeper on the right ways to build a modern sales tech stack, we tapped a few of our subject matter experts and customers. The first is Chad Dyar, Director of Sales Enablement at OnDeck. Chad has built and managed tech stacks for multiple fast-growth companies and has developed an active/passive approach to building a stack for his team.

The Active/Passive Approach

According to Chad, active tools require a behavioral change from the sales team. Passive tools generally run on the backend enhancing the enablement team's processes without requiring any additional effort from sales. When building out a tech stack, alternating between these types of tools keeps the sales team from being overwhelmed with change while maintaining momentum on the technical side of sales improvement initiatives.

The hardest part about building a tech stack for a sales organization who is new to sales tools is change management. Driving adoption requires buy-in, and getting buy-in is easier when it comes from reaction to feedback. The approach of "Here's this cool thing that is going to make you more money" sounds nice, but disrupting a performing sales team's current process without everyone on board with the change is a setup for failure.

Chad's Take: Choosing the First New Tool

How do you choose the first new tool? Find the friction.

The first tool of the tech stack is the foundation for what's to come. It is important to choose a tool that alleviates some form of universal friction. When I say universal, I mean that Sales, Sales Management, Rev Ops, and Enablement are all feeling the pain. Our specific example of friction was call coaching. We were doing it, but it was painful and inconsistent. Calls were hard to pull and often chosen at random, and call notes were kept in a spreadsheet. Sales did not have a clear path for areas of improvement. The process was so time-consuming that managers had to spend time outside of business hours preparing to coach calls. Rev Ops was not able to leverage the quality of conversations as a metric for driving funnel conversions. Enablement did not have consistent and measurable examples of opportunities to leverage for onboarding for ongoing sales trainings. A tool that would set the organization up for better coaching had universal appeal. When the first tool solves an immediate need, it sets everyone up for long-term success.

What's the ROI?

In a customer-centric environment, it is critical to create engagement and consistency in the sales process in a way that drives desired business outcomes—that is, "Show me the money." We needed a tool to investigate why customers gave certain salespeople rave reviews and to understand what "great" sounded like on the phone. We also needed to ensure that managers could coach their teams in a way that demonstrated improvements both in the quality of calls and in the quantity of converted opportunities. All of this became trackable with a coaching tool. When selling a tool internally (especially the first one), it's important to tie the expected results back to company goals. Growing revenue is generally at the top. Our return on investment (ROI) statement included how we intended to leverage coaching (and subsequent training) to improve conversions, customer experience, and manager effectiveness.

How Do We Drive Adoption at All Levels?

The process for driving adoption was to give everyone a role to play in the success of the first tool. After the tool is implemented and training is complete, expectations and timelines have to be set and accountability put into place. For our first tool, we had salespeople pull specific types of calls, score them, and share them with their managers. Managers then listened, notated, and scored the calls as well. The managers met with each member of their team once a week for a call coaching session. We tracked improvements through our sales enablement technology to learn what was working and what wasn't. Weekly call coaching became the new normal when everyone clearly understood what was expected of them. Coaching became part of the job. To continue the momentum of coaching, we layered in contests like the "Coaching Olympics" and "Call of the Month" to keep excitement around the new tool going. At the end of the day, salespeople are better on the phone, managers are becoming better coaches, and Enablement has deep insights into opportunities for improving the quality of conversations. The wins all around set up an adaptive environment.

What Does Success Look Like?

Successfully adopting a tool changes the culture. If the tool feels like "one more thing" everyone has to do, results are mediocre at best. There are several tell-tale signs that the culture has changed. For example, you hear mention of buzzwords more frequently. In our case, everyone is talking about "coaching." Managers and teams are competing with one another in every category of our coaching scorecards. Who is the best relationship builder? The best closer? Who is the best at overcoming objections/competition? Managers who coach teams with great scorecards are the go-to coaches on the floor. Executive leaders have easy access to data supporting insights on how the actual "sales" part of inside sales is progressing.

Before a tool goes live, if you can have success clearly defined with key stakeholders, you will have a better understanding of whether you have overcome the point of friction successfully.

Keep It Moving

While the sales teams and managers were buzzing about coaching, Enablement implemented a second "passive" lead routing tool that drastically improved the way we are able to segment and route leads to our teams. Tool number two did not require any behavioral changes for the sales team.

Sales gets tools to optimize their process over a timeline that does not feel like "too much change," and the addition of the passive tools keeps Enablement busy supporting an infrastructure designed to create a better sales culture, a friction-light sales process, and a revenue-driving machine.

Another Way to Look at It

According to the *Harvard Business Review*, the number of people involved in business-to-business (B2B) solutions purchases has climbed from an average of 5.4 people in 2015 to 6.8 people in 2017. Now I don't know who that 0.8 of a person is, but let's unpack this statement a bit. In B2B transactions, the decision to purchase something new, whether it be software, hardware, advertising, or a team lunch order, is done by committee. Multiple people weigh in on the decision throughout the business.

This is why, as mentioned earlier, you need a multichannel approach in order to engage your full buying committee. The only way to be omnichannel at scale is to have a modern tech stack.

Unpacking this further, if you are a sales and marketing team trying to educate a company to make a purchase decision, you need to reach all seven (or 6.8) of those people within the organization with your message. Then, on top of that, it requires numerous repetitions before someone will recall your message, and now we are just swimming in numbers.

The Marketing Rule of Seven states that a prospect needs to "hear" the advertiser's message at least seven times before they'll take an action to buy that product or service. It's a marketing maxim developed by the movie industry in the 1930s. Studio bosses discovered that a certain amount of advertising and promotion was required to compel someone to see one of their movies.

Today, our Outreach data show us that it can take anywhere from eight to 20 touches to garner a response when it comes to cold prospecting.

Overall, the message is pretty clear: To be successful in selling in a B2B context, you need a coordinated campaign that reaches and engages multiple people within an organization. Thankfully, modern sales and marketing technology are here to assist. To help, we brought in Jessica Cross, Manager, Demand Generation, at a prominent high-growth AdTech company.

Jessica's campaigns are well-orchestrated, sophisticated marketing motions incorporating multichannel touches, personalization at scale, Account-based Marketing, and optimizing for the buyer's journey, just to name a few elements.

Let's look at an actual example of how a client responds to a highly coordinated campaign. In this e-mail, Jessica has a head of a department asking her team to sign up for an event. The respondent remarks that she

Hi all,

I received the below invitation for an event which takes place at Oceana on Tuesday, Oct. 23, from 9am - 11am. It looks interesting and very relevant to our Inverta project recommendations, so I thought I'd pass on to you, and if you're interested in attending, you can register using the details in the email below.

Here's a slide deck I found for an event they did previously, which is worth a look.

I also received an invitation to this in the mail (hello, multi-channel marketing) and had never had any interactions with us before, so maybe they know what they're doing!

Thanks,
Elizabeth

Figure 10.1 A Client Response to a Well-coordinated Campaign

has had other interactions with the brand, including a printed invite in the mail with the same message. This is smooth orchestration at its finest. According to Jessica, "This is the Holy Grail of multichannel messaging that is possible only with a modern tech stack."

Here is what happened behind the scenes. Jessica's motion included:

- Identifying a key list of companies within her CRM
- Syncing that list of companies to their advertising platform for display ads
- Syncing people within those companies into their SEP, allowing sales reps to send e-mail invites
- Syncing people to their Marketing Automation platform so they could send attractive visual e-mail invites
- Integrating a direct mail vendor within CRM, allowing reps to ship physical invites on demand

Isn't modern marketing grand? This is a beautiful example of a well-orchestrated marketing campaign that takes full advantage of a modern tech stack to create a high-quality buyer experience.

Want to take a cue from Jessica? Here's what you'll need:

Tech Stack Essentials for a Flawless Omnichannel Campaign

- CRM
- Digital Advertising platform
- SEP
- Marketing Automation platform
- Direct mail

Key Features to Look For

- Predictive intelligence (data and scoring)
- Data augmentation
- Multitouch attribution
- Personalization or predictive content on site

Jessica remarks, "If you're feeling like this is a lot to manage, no mention to pay for, you are not alone. For that, I have a couple of recommendations."

To minimize the burden, she suggests finding complementary solutions that easily integrate across your existing technology suite to make onboarding a new solution less painful. She also adds that true revenue attribution is a must. "Never choose a product that can't truly tie to dollars earned—it's not worth the price of admission," Jessica states.

"For example, let's say you implement an A/B testing tool on your website and improve landing page conversion rates by 3 percentage points. Congratulations!" Jessica says.

"But what if you aren't seeing your retention rates and lifetime value improve as a result of those increased click-throughs? Worse, what if you can't even know what happened beyond the click? This is why you have to bypass pure activity and top-of-funnel metrics in favor of true revenue attribution."

"When investing in a new software, it is more important to evaluate the potential ROI, not the sticker price. If you have to spend $4,000 instead of $2,000 to make $40,000, the upfront investment is well worth it."

—*Jessica Cross, Manager, Demand Generation, at a prominent high-growth AdTech company*

To be able to accurately measure today's sophisticated marketing campaigns, you need a modern tech stack that integrates from the top of your funnel to the bottom.

Matches Made in Revenue Heaven: Perfect Pairings for Full-Funnel Attribution

- Visual website optimizer + Heap Analytics
- Segment + Customer.io
- Outreach + Bizible
- Marketo + Salesforce
- QuickBooks + Revel

Lastly, Jessica advises against bargain shopping when it comes to technology. Although it may be tempting to pick a core tool that has the lowest cost, it won't be very useful if it doesn't have easy integration or low-funnel attribution.

Jessica's Quick and Dirty Platform Feature Checklist

- API endpoints
- App stores and marketplaces
- Closed-loop reporting and revenue attribution

Now we're really seeing the omnichannel approach in action!

Sales Engagement Has Become the *Must-have* Line Item

As we talk about the sales stack, and the modern sales technologies that exist or are being built to help the modern seller adhere to how the modern buyer likes to buy, we can't help but keep coming back to Sales Engagement.

Sales Engagement is the center of this universe. CRM is an interchangeable data warehouse. Data services provide data that can be found just about anywhere these days. But when it comes to engaging with your customers and prospects, a platform that provides access to multiple communication channels, provides analytics to perform tests and share best practices across the team, provides the next best action to take, works seamlessly with the rest of your tech stack, and allows your team to do it together, that's the true heart of your sales process.

What to Know When Implementing a Sales Engagement Platform

No modern sales tech stack is complete without a modern SEP.

A Sales Engagement platform accelerates *all* activities, so it's quite powerful. With great power comes great responsibility. Snippets, templates, and sequences shrink the time it takes to write messages. Tasks, scheduled sends, and sequences keep the flow of messages marching forward in an orchestrated fashion.

Meetings functionality allows your customers to schedule time efficiently, and premium voice features ensure that your conversations are documented and can even be analyzed for coaching opportunities.

Executed properly, a Sales Engagement implementation in your sales organization is like a beautiful symphony. But every symphony requires a thoughtful selection of musicians, with their instruments tuned to the perfect pitch.

To guide you through a fully optimized implementation, we turned to Alex Greer, an Outreach customer since July 2015. Alex previously ran Global Sales Enablement at two of the fastest-growing software companies of all time, Medallia and Cloudera, and now he runs his own firm called Signal HQ. He's personally taught hundreds of sales reps how to use SEPs to accelerate their sales motions. Along the way, he's learned a thing or two about what works and where things can go awry.

Here's how Alex runs a successful SEP implementation.

Alex's Take: Starting with Your Stakeholders

First, let's identify who should be involved in the decision-making process at every step of your journey. The key stakeholders are:

- **Frontline and Second-Line Sales Managers.** This role is responsible for reporting and enforcing process with Outreach. For each part of your sales organization using Outreach, every Frontline Manager and their manager must be involved in the conversation. If this is not possible, nominate someone who has full authority to speak and decide on behalf of all the others.
- **Sales Operations.** This role is responsible for administering Outreach. Sales Ops is often solely responsible for implementation and training coordination and is the first tier of internal support for users.
- **Marketing Operations.** This role is responsible for monitoring progress and opportunity conversion of all marketing-generated

leads. Marketing Ops will be most interested in reporting capability and standardization of messages.

- **At least two or three top tech-oriented Individual Contributors (SDRs/BDRs and/or AEs/AMs).** This role is the end user of your SEP. Once it goes live in your organization, they will spend a large chunk of their time using this platform as their core source of communication with prospects and customers. It is imperative that this role has a seat at the table. You'll be surprised by this role's deep working knowledge of your systems, identifying gaps or opportunities for efficiency that managers and Operations may have missed. Another added benefit is that by including them, you will foster their trust and gain buy-in and ultimately a groundswell of support rather than stubborn resistance.

A Step-by-step Approach

Step 1: CRM Mapping for Orchestration and Reporting

Here's the thing: You don't just turn on an SEP and start using it. You defeat most of the major purpose of the investment if you do that. Outreach's power lies in its ability to seamlessly document and coordinate your sales organization's activities into your single source of truth: CRM.

Key decisions to make:

Accounts
Fields to sync
- Which one's map to standard Outreach fields?
- Which should map to custom fields?

Account creation
- Should an account created in Outreach sync to CRM?

Leads and contacts
Fields to sync
- Which one's map to standard Outreach fields?
- Which should map to custom fields?

Prospect creation

- Should a prospect created in Outreach sync to CRM?
- Should it be created as a lead or contact?
- Two-way or one-way sync of edits? (Ask this about every single field.)
- Document an agreed-upon process in the event of duplicate records

Step 2: Sequence Strategy for Optimizing Conversion

Sequences are used by SDRs/BDRs in three distinct ways:

- Inbound lead follow-up
- Outbound prospecting
- Event invitations

Meanwhile, your AEs and Account Managers (AMs) can leverage sequences for the following:

- Opportunity (new, renewal, or expand) progression follow-up reminders
- Expansion opportunities with new potential stakeholders in the account

It's essential to arrive at a standard "plan of attack" with each type of sequence so you can efficiently run, measure, and fine-tune your team's touchpoints and messaging as a whole.

The best sequences include a variety of touchpoints (100% templated e-mails, semitemplated e-mails with an opportunity to customize, phone calls, and engagement via LinkedIn or other social media) across a specific period of time.

For inbound leads, response time is a crucial factor. In all cases, the number of touchpoints, and the space of time between those touchpoints, is important to specify. Make sure you're automating inbound sequences to optimize quick follow-ups. If your organization has standardized its fields for specific lead sources, you can take your automation to the next level. That's why it's incredibly important to have crystal-clear definitions processed around lead and contact statuses.

SEP sequences can automatically change lead/contact statuses as they are added to, advanced, and finished through a sequence. This is phenomenal for marketing and inside sales reporting visibility but can wreak chaos if a process is not defined and adhered to.

Be sure to set up a *trigger* to detect a specific *lead source detail* in your CRM and launch a corresponding sequence specific to that lead source in Outreach. This solves the follow-up response time issue.

Step 3: Automation Versus Customization for Increasing Output

This is a critical philosophical question every organization must make: How much "freedom of expression" do you allow your individual contributors with their sequences? Rather than suggesting exactly what to do, engage in a roundtable question where you all ask the following questions:

- How much more likely will our customer respond to a personalized message versus a general one?
- Does a message need to be 100% personalized, or can it be role-, industry-, or account-specific?
- How much productivity (number of people contacted in a given period of time) is an individual contributor willing to sacrifice in the name of customization?
- In the event that we feel an automated, templated message isn't working, how quickly can we identify it and agree on a revision?

Step 4: Task Prioritization for Efficiency

SEPs should not feel like a 100%, fully automated system. They should also provide a variety of reminders in the form of tasks to communicate with your prospects.

The best way to execute tasks efficiently is by "chunking" them into groups. Among your team, agree on an approach that works best for your business.

Some suggestions include:

- By task type (inbound sequence call tasks, open e-mail call tasks, manual e-mails, etc.)
- By account
- By role
- By industry
- By product

Step 5: Smart Views for Organization

You will quickly rack up hundreds and thousands of contacts and accounts in your SEP instance. Smart views are a great way to organize them quickly.

Recommended uses include:

- Grouping by key fields that are missing or need to be updated (account assignment, title, stage, e-mail address, phone number, LinkedIn URL)
- Grouping by role
- Grouping by prospect stage

Step 6: The Key Factors Necessary for E-mail Deliverability

Your team's use of an SEP can grind to a halt if you run into deliverability issues. This is what happens when you misuse a powerful tool! It's up to you as a sales leader to put a process in place to keep these key factors under control (after all, that's what this book is for!).

- Quantity of e-mails: Gmail has a daily send limit of approximately 2,000 e-mails per user per day. Make sure no individual person is adding so many prospects to their sequences that this limit could be exceeded.

- Throttling: Many companies have spam filters that detect if an individual is sending e-mails to numerous members of their org in rapid succession. Outreach's throttling feature does a great job of managing e-mail sends so you don't get flagged as spam or blocked altogether. I always found their reps knowledgeable about recommendations on throttle settings.

- Open-and-click tracking: The more tracking pixels in your e-mail, the more likely your e-mail will be blocked. E-mail open tracking is generally not enough to get blocked, so turn that on unless something goes awry. Keep link tracking turned off unless your organization feels it is critical for a link to be tracked within an e-mail (such as an event invite).

- Embedding images and attaching files: This is another factor that can get your e-mail blocked. Keep the text-to-image ratio to a minimum of 70:30, and refrain from attachments (especially large ones) as much as possible.

- Bounced e-mails: Your company's domain reputation is affected by your delivered-to-bounced ratio. Set up processes to ensure that bounced e-mails are quickly scrubbed or corrected, and invest in contact databases that have a proven track record and process for maintaining e-mail accuracy only. If paying for data, this is not an area to skimp to save a few cents. Bad data can come back to haunt you later.

Step 7: Testing for Smooth Performance (and to Save Yourself from Embarrassment)

Test *everything* before launching!

When first implementing your SEP, start by manually loading content into templates and sending to yourself or a colleague. Check that the sequence runs smoothly and the appearance of text and images in your e-mails look correct. Look to coordinate with your SEP customer success rep if you run into questions or issues.

When composing *any* new template, click the Preview button and send yourself a test e-mail *first*. This is the best way to catch grammar, spelling, punctuation, and formatting errors.

For extra safety, I like to read test e-mails on a mobile phone. A majority of your recipients will read the e-mail alert on their phone and open it there first. You will be amazed at the opportunities for improvement that you notice when reading on a phone versus a desktop.

Step 8: Expand Your Templates for Broader Communication Use Cases

Setting up your initial sequences is only the beginning! Before long, you'll be expanding and fine-tuning. This is a great place to start getting creative and working with other revenue orgs.

For example:

- Ask your team to contribute to a library of follow-up *snippets* to shortcut their communications. A contest is usually the best way to get people to volunteer for this.
- Create persona-specific sequences with marketing. One for ice-cold, never-been-contacted outreach and another for follow-ups to folks who responded in the past but didn't convert.
- Create invite sequences for your upcoming events and webinars.
- And so much more!

Your Sales Engagement Platform Evaluation Checklist

Don't invest in just any SEP. Make sure to get one that's set up to scale with your growth and will continue to innovate with what's technically possible. Here's a handy checklist for evaluating a modern SEP:

- Reliable and secure
- Easy to use and administer
- CRM and inbox integrations
- Omnichannel ecosystem integrations
- Systematic engagement
- Activity-based analytics and revenue attribution

- Integrated meeting support and calendaring
- Seamless talk
- Texting support
- LinkedIn integration
- Prospect intelligence
- Task workflow and prioritization
- Increment-based sequence steps
- Bulk action
- Rapid inbound lead handling
- Smart salesforce sync and opportunity engagement
- E-mail safeguards
- GDPR-ready
- Predictive support
- Hires developers from proven companies like Microsoft, Amazon, etc.
- Works with global companies who are hyperfocused on security like Amazon Web Services, Red Hat, or Cloudera

As Alex previously stated, modern SEPs are powerful tools. Take your time to set them up right and train your team properly, and you'll reap endless benefits. Once it's up and running, it's all about driving teamwide adoption.

A Key Element of Adoption Is Empathy

"You can't have innovation without adoption, and you can't have adoption without empathy."

—Mario Espinoza, Sales Operations Manager at Outreach

Our very own Mario Espinoza, Sales Operations Manager at Outreach, describes his process-building and implementation experience eloquently, saying, "After 15 years of operational experience, I realized I was wrong. What was I wrong about? That question can only be answered by one phrase, 'Empathy drives innovation.'"

Mario describes how, over the course of his career, he, like so many of his technology counterparts, focused heavily on driving adoption so that clients could have a world-class user experience. Sounds pretty noble, right?

But here's where Mario says he went wrong: He failed to understand that empathy toward his clients must first start with empathy toward his own colleagues, the customer-facing teams at Outreach. Sounds pretty basic, right? According to Mario, as basic as it seems, he has seen countless numbers of new initiatives, products, and tools fail to gain adoption simply because the starting point for empathy is for the external customer instead of the internal one.

Ensuring quick and thorough adoption is critical in the current business climate, which encompasses fierce competition and increasing pressure to scale. Automation, custom software, and the vast number of technical vendors allow companies to move quickly and gain traction. Many operational leaders understand that with speed comes the challenge of executing on creating *successful repeatable* processes. Consistency in this regard opens up opportunity for an economy of scale many companies are looking for.[1] Pairing the new key piece of data, technology, or process with the right empathetic approach can dramatically streamline time to value and gain sustained adoption.

Here are Mario's three tips for creating repeatable processes with an "empathetic innovation" mindset.

Mario's Take: A Sales Ops Manager's Secrets for Swift Adoption

Shadow Often

At Outreach, our customer-facing teams are part of the process of any new implementation. Feedback loops, focus groups, and effective trainings are always part of the standard implementation process and should be table

---

[1] https://www.forbes.com/sites/theyec/2016/11/30/how-to-build-consistency-and-accountability-into-your-sales-process/#3fe7c6214fd1

stakes. However, this is not enough. That's why our Operations teams take it one step further by systematically shadowing teams. For clarity, shadowing is simply taking time to follow a salesperson's day-to-day activities. This effort has proven to yield extremely positive results because it:

- Provides clear insights into how systems and processes are *actually* used, giving Operations teams a better understanding of the downstream impact on the user.
- Fosters an atmosphere of collaboration and innovation. When everyone is involved and shares in the ownership, adoption is an almost automatic result.
- Encourages Operations teams to rethink the value of a product, process, or technology away from their own personal choice—the antithesis of empathy—to one with an empathetic lens.

Some years ago, I had the opportunity to work for a company that had missed its revenue goals. My primary charge was to operationally support a sales team that was responsible for the growth of our client's small business by leveraging our product. The technology, data, and tools available were outstanding. Yet, for some reason, revenue goals were missed. As part of my normal process, I would not only shadow, but I would also pick one or two days per week and do my work in their area. The presence of an operational partner was immediately met with a bit of surprise and excitement. Immediately, our teams began to build a road map for adoption with an empathetic focus on our sales teams and to address the challenges they were facing.

As I shadowed one sales rep—let's call him Joe—I was shocked to see that he created a very manual but interesting account scoring system model in a spreadsheet. After watching him enter in information coupled with the amount of accounts on the sheet, it was clear to me that more time was being spent on manual tracking and ranking than the actual conversations and connections with clients. By operationalizing this really creative ranking model into an automated workflow, activity tripled and sales increased 200% in the first month alone. Moreover, there was heightened engagement with sales teams because their ideas were being heard and implemented, allowing the company to make a huge leap in Revenue Efficiency.

Revisit Implementations

My personal favorite part of this three-step process is revisiting any previous implementations on a consistent basis (I know, I'm a such a true Operations nerd!). There are several reasons why this step has proven to be a key step—the most important is the learning that happens. This is where the iterative process takes center stage. A perfect example of this is Amazon, who attributes their dedication and focus on being an iterative company as a large part of their success to date.

On a subtler note, by planning with an iterative process in mind, it sends a message that perfection is not the goal but rather the learnings in the successes and failures. Once this becomes a consistent practice, the fear of failure disappears, cross-functionally bringing teams together. We see this practice today with many companies and their version of a "hack week," where teams can come together and work on projects they choose. From my experience, revisiting is the catalyst to much of the larger innovations that can happen within a company.

An example of this was at a multimedia advertising company I worked for. Our company generated leads from their website by consumers needing service providers. Our company would then forward the leads to the providers. A mobile app was created to speed up response times. The intent was to reduce time spent by salespeople coaching providers and increase time focused on sales conversations. This worked as intended for about four months. After some time, salespeople reverted to primarily coaching and less on sales. Interestingly enough, one of those sales reps had put together the idea of the company answering those leads immediately and then providing a warm transfer to the first-available provider. After an implementation review, the solution was implemented and became one of the company's largest revenue drivers, reducing churn and exponentially increasing sales velocity.

Close the Loop

The old adage "Communication is a two-way street" is core to this empathetic perspective. Creating pathways for feedback is only part of the equation. Before coming to Outreach, I had the opportunity to connect with some of Outreach's employees to talk about what it was like to work there. One of the most impressive pieces of feedback I received was how Outreach employees at all levels took feedback directly from customers and iterated on the product quickly. This created a very loyal client base that saw success and wanted to be part of the improvement process. This approach permeated the company atmosphere and led to the fast release schedule Outreach currently follows. Additionally, this also had an impact on the culture at Outreach. Employees can and do provide feedback, and the company acts swiftly, solidifying company core values. As Ops professionals, it is our responsibility to build our feedback loop between ourselves and internal clients.

What If I'm Just Getting Started?

If you're part of a large company, feel free to read on, but for those of you at smaller orgs wondering how to get started, we've got something for you.

Our very own Scott Barker, Head of Partnerships for Sales Hacker, built his first sales tech stack at his first startup, which helped him add $10 million in qualified pipeline. Here's how he did it.

Scott's Take: Make a List of the Challenges You're Solving for

This may sound obvious, but trust me, when you're sitting in demo after demo with an overly excited AE pitching you on every feature under the sun, your end goals will start to get blurry. Make sure you have your list on-hand at all times to refer back to.

My personal challenge list looked something like this:

1. Our team needs better data.
2. We need a way to make more phone calls and send more personalized e-mails.
3. My SDRs need to stand out from the crowd.
4. I need a record of all the interactions and a way to ensure that everyone is following our process.

Good Artists Copy, Great Artists Steal

You don't have to feel stressed to reinvent the wheel. Find successful companies in your city that are at a similar growth stage or slightly beyond and set up some coffee dates.

After dozens of coffee dates (and phone calls), here are the four main categories that made my list:

1. CRM (we went with Salesforce): Bye-bye, challenge 4!
2. Sales Engagement (Outreach.io, of course!): Go ahead and check off challenges 2, 3, and 4!
3. Data source (we came away with ZoomInfo, LeadIQ, and DiscoverOrg): See you later, challenge 1!
4. Social tools (LinkedIn Sales Navigator was the clear winner here): More love for challenge 1 and 3!

Implement, Measure, and Iterate

Once you've overlaid your challenges with your learnings from the other orgs you spoke with, it's time to make some decisions and move forward with the implementation. It's time to test your hypothesis that these are the right tools for your org.

My learnings from the onboarding process and beyond:

1. Technology solutions live and die by how effectively they are implemented—do not cut corners here! Be the annoying client who takes full advantage of ALL the training sessions. No training offered? 90% of tools will have an online training platform of some sort.
2. Talk with your CSM to get some benchmarks and set up KPIs accordingly so that you can measure the effectiveness of each tool.
3. Set up monthly technology stack reviews and block off time to research/preview new technology that's coming to market (first adopters can have a huge advantage).
4. Once you're comfortable with your stack, you can start to add in other, more complex layers.

What's Still to Come

Having done partnerships for Sales Hacker, I've worked with more than 120 different sales vendors in the past year alone. These are my workflows to look out for in the near future:

- Task workflow and prioritization: With the role of an AE/SDR becoming more and more complex with each passing quarter, workflow and prioritization are a must in order for leadership to easily see that the highest priority accounts/leads are getting the attention they need. Smart efficiency will be the name of the game here. Next best action is coming soon.
- Smart syncs and triggers: Your stack will need to work harmoniously together, and high-performing teams will have all their different data sources aggregated so that the broader orgs can benefit from the real-time learnings taking place in all the systems. Your platforms should also have automatic, built-in triggers that don't require manual action from your reps in order to increase speed to engagement.
- Intelligence: To make each and every engagement positive, reps will need insights being served up to them live, in the tools that they already use every day. I'd keep a close eye on "conversational intelligence" platforms as well; they are proving to be a game changer for reps.

- Video: I don't see anything that has the power to humanize a rep
  faster than video. Having implemented video into my own process,
  I've seen my sales interactions become increasingly positive throughout the entire funnel. The best companies are finding creative ways
  to utilize video before it becomes table stakes.

This brings us to our next chapter, where we predict what's
happening next in sales.

Chapter 11

Predicting What's Next in Sales

E fficiency is key. As global financial markets fluctuate, creating an organization focused on Revenue Efficiency will keep you in business and in the game no matter how bad it gets. This is why it's imperative to set your business up for success now. If and when things do deflate with the global markets, you will be set up to run a lean, mean, revenue-generating, low-cash-burning machine.

This is also why it's important to think ahead. In sales, we forecast our numbers. It's our way to think and plan ahead. In this book, we had full chapters dedicated to omnichannel outreach, A/B testing and next best actions to take, Revenue Efficiency, revenue org alignment, humanization at scale, and much more. That's because not only are these pieces of the modern sales process relevant now, but they're also mainstays of the future of sales. We are still in the very early stages of Sales Engagement. The innovators and early adopters get it, but we haven't crossed the chasm yet!

We gave Jake Dunlap, CEO of Skaled, a leading Sales Engagement implementation consulting firm, a crystal ball and said, "Shake it up!" Here's where he thinks the future of sales is going.

Jake's Take: The Future of Sales

The way we engage in B2B sales is evolving at an incredible pace.

Until the late 2000s, the primary methods for engaging were phone, events, and direct mail, and maybe a little fax as well. E-mail then started to evolve from being a primarily consumer application to a B2B communication. Finally, Marketing Automation emerged as a sector and took off.

In 2014, we started to see this technology filter over to the sales floor, and the results were amazing. We stopped calling as much when e-mail started to work like nothing we had seen before. Generic e-mails with custom objects worked at an alarming rate, so why make people call?

Today, e-mail is becoming more and more saturated, and we are seeing reply rates at all-time lows. The amount of personalization needed now to cut through the noise is becoming an issue for SDR and sales executives who were brought up with the mantra of "more" as a metric versus "more and better" are having to learn that nuance. As we look forward, sales and marketing leaders are now being forced to rethink the way they are building and scaling their outbound efforts to track different metrics, as well as volume around e-mail in particular.

So, what is working and what does the future hold for everyone looking to be proactive with their outbound efforts? There are four trends that Jake feels are going to be critical through 2020 and beyond, ones that every outbound team needs to be prepared for.

Phone Skills Will Be Critical Again

We got out of the habit of having people pick up the phone, and frankly, it was the right thing to do because e-mail was working at scale. Now, I think we'll need to go back to the phone as a mainstay of outreach because it's just not being used as much. Therefore, there's less noise.

Those who are using cold calls as an outbound sales technique are seeing significant business advantages. According to a DiscoverOrg survey, 55% of high-growth companies—those who experienced a minimum of 40% growth over the previous three years—stated that cold calling is very much alive. The survey also determined that the companies who said cold calling is dead experienced 42% less growth than those who said it was alive.

I believe the lack of calling is also why we're seeing longer ramp times for SDRs to make the transition to sales roles. This is because they aren't used to actually talking to people and dealing with objections.

LinkedIn Will Be a Primary Channel

Right now, LinkedIn direct messages feel a lot like e-mail back in 1998: poised for explosion. In the coming years, more and more teams are going to wise up to the fact that so few messages are being sent through this channel and LinkedIn for sales and for marketing will emerge as major channels for their respective organizations. The other LinkedIn trend we will see is individual reps and leaders building their own networks of people in industries that they can activate or get referrals from in the future. More and more people will become thought leaders in the Internet of Things, Sales, or whatever space and then become a trusted advisor to that network. Yes, the influencer marketing that is prevalent on LinkedIn now will be much more formalized and built into the architecture by 2020. Remember, people tend to trust subject matter experts over speaking to sales reps directly.

Omnichannel Is Required

As we look to the future, e-mailing and calling only—no matter how customized your outreach is—will not be enough.

Direct mail is making a comeback as we yearn for something new that thinks outside our crammed inboxes. The reason many B2B companies don't use direct mail is logistics, but more and more software solutions are emerging to remove that friction. LinkedIn will be a primary channel for all the reasons I just stated. Events will continue to be a great way to activate offline conversations and communications. I think the impact of webinars will shrink as we get inundated with hundreds of webinar choices every month, so we will most likely do more on-demand, online content sharing like Instagram, Facebook, and YouTube Live. People will want less friction in the process, and these formats are all frictionless.

Removing Friction for the Seller Will Be Paramount

When we think of removing friction, we are often referencing the buyer experience (and rightly so). But another major trend will be removing friction for the seller. In the future, all of the same communication methods (e-mail, phone, social media, video, etc.) will still be in play. It is less about reinventing the wheel and more about supercharging what's under the hood.

Technology solutions that augment your seller's current selling tools and supercharge them with more seamlessness, speed, customization, and scale will rule the day.

For smaller businesses, this can mean handy features like Gmail Add-ons and Chrome extensions that allow you to supercharge your efforts and remain right in your inbox. For companies that are competing at a larger scale, SEPs allow reps to manage their full communication stack—text, phone calls, LinkedIn, e-mail, etc.—from a single platform. This cuts down on the mental cost of context switching between platforms and also provides a powerful centralized view of communication activity. Reps can unpack an entire buyer's journey and see at a glance which technology medium was most effective and what time of day was most likely to result in contact, and they can also personalize their communications using sales intelligence provided right in the platform. This single console experience will be the future, and the days of logging in and out in different tools all day will be extinct.

In other words, the biggest trend through 2020 and beyond is that the days of "more for more's sake" are coming to an end. The SDR or salesperson of tomorrow will indeed have to deliver an incredible volume to compete—but mediocrity at scale is still mediocrity. Instead, the sales force of tomorrow will have to scale and also be smarter, more customized, and scrappier than ever before to gain a true competitive advantage.

Jake had a way of thinking about the future of sales that is very well aligned with how we're thinking about the Sales Engagement movement and the channels given to us, but what about a whole new approach for a whole new type of audience? One focused on the ways these *new* entrants to the workforce, and soon to be decision makers, like to operate?

As consumers, our attention spans have gotten shorter, our aptitude and interest in technology has grown, and our expectations are higher— we want stuff to just work. This is only increasing as Millennials and Gen Z individuals enter the workforce. As mentioned earlier in the book, these folks are native to social networks, the iPhone, texting, and photo sharing apps. That's not stopping anytime soon.

Modern consumers want product design to be so flawless, so intuitive, so slick that we can just use it. In answer to these buyer expectations, we are in the midst of a movement to revolutionize Sales Engagement and lead with the product. Companies like Dropbox, Atlassian, Expensify, and Slack are at the forefront, but you too should be considering how product-led growth strategies can impact your business.

What is product-led growth? We invited Liz Cain, VP of Go-to-Market at OpenView Partners, to lead us through it.

Company	Enterprise Value (EV)	CY2018E Revenue	CY2018E Revenue Growth Rate	TTM Gross Margin
Atlassian (NASDAQ:TEAM)	$13,717	$864	39.3%	80.2%
Shopify (NYSE:SHOP)	$13,706	$1,032	53.3%	56.5%
Dropbox (NASDAQ:DBX)	$12,305	$1,357	24.1%	66.3%
DocuSign (NASDAQ:DOCU)	$8,570	$656	26.5%	73.4%
New Relic (NYSE:NEWR)	$5,697	$585	36.0%	70.1%
Zendesk (NASDAQ:ZEN)	$5,435	$463	30.3%	82.3%
LogMeIn (NASDAQ:LOGM)	$5,391	$1,191	20.3%	78.2%
Twilio (NYSE:TWLO)	$5,057	$588	47.5%	53.4%
Wix (NASDAQ:WIX)	$4,602	$599	40.6%	81.3%
HubSpot (NYSE:HUBS)	$4,575	$498	32.7%	80.2%
Pluralsight (NASDAQ:PS)	$3,146	$224	34.2%	70.3%
Smartsheet (NYSE:SMAR)	$2,524	$161	44.9%	80.4%
MongoDB (NASDAQ:MDB)	$2,242	$220	42.2%	72.2%
SendGrid (NYSE:SEND)	$1,007	$144	28.4%	74.2%
PLG Index Median	$5,224	$587	35.1%	73.8%
SaaS Index Median	$2,304	$257	25.3%	69.9%

CY2018E EBITDA Margin	EV/Revenue	CY2018E Rule of 40	S&M Expense as Percent of 2017 Revenue	R&D Expense as Percent of 2017 Revenue
28.0%	15.9x	67.8%	21.8%	50.0%
3.3%	13.3x	56.7%	33.5%	20.2%
21.3%	9.1x	81.9%	29.7%	34.3%
5.1%	13.1x	31.6%	53.6%	17.8%
6.8%	9.7x	42.8%	51.3%	26.8%
12.6%	11.8x	42.9%	58.3%	20.9%
36.7%	4.5x	57.0%	35.1%	15.8%
3.7%	8.6x	51.2%	25.2%	30.3%
18.6%	7.7x	59.2%	48.0%	36.1%
9.4%	9.2x	42.1%	56.7%	18.7%
-21.8%	14.1x	12.4%	62.0%	29.5%
-31.2%	15.7x	13.7%	65.5%	33.8%
-31.8%	10.2x	10.4%	71.2%	40.3%
12.8%	7.0x	41.2%	25.2%	26.5%
8.1%	10.0x	42.8%	49.7%	28.2%
9.6%	7.7x	37.0%	43.5%	19.4%

Figure 11.1 Product–led Growth Index[1]

[1] https://openviewpartners.com/product-led-growth-index/

To Liz, product-led growth is, first and foremost, a go-to-market strategy that puts the product at the center of your customer experience—from customer acquisition to adoption, retention, and expansion. When compared to the broader set of public SaaS companies, product-led growth companies grow faster, trade at higher multiples, and are double.

Liz's Take: Why The Future is Product-Led

The way we engage with buyers is changing—fast. But *product-led* does not mean *product only*, and even traditional enterprise companies are looking for ways to delabor the sales process in order to meet the demands of today's buyers. To better understand the current state of software sales, it's important to get a handle on our past. Over the past 40 years, we have seen many iterations of go-to-market in software, from field sales to inside sales to the rise of content marketing and sales automation.

In the 1980s and early 1990s, companies like Oracle, PTC, and IBM mastered the field sales model. They built enormous, aggressive field sales forces that spent most of their time on the road, building relationships in person in order to close very large contracts.

Fast-forward to 2000, and the first true cloud businesses needed to get sellers off the road in order to compete with these behemoths in a cost-effective way. Salesforce was one of the first out of the gate with an inside model. They demonstrated a consistent ability to scale with an outbound sales team in those early years—and proved that telesales could win a high close rate at one-third the cost and in one-third the amount of the time as the traditional selling model.

A decade later, as the inside sales model was broadly adopted, we discovered that we needed to play the volume game and target a large number of prospects while minimizing the highly manual (and expensive!) process of sales reps cold calling. Many companies pursued a strategy of specialization and built outbound SDR teams made of less expensive and often more junior sales team members, but the most efficient answer lay with marketing and inbound demand. We saw all kinds of creative approaches to driving awareness and inbound lead flow with a particular focus on the rise of content marketing.

In each evolution of software go-to-market, you'll notice that more and more of the sales reps' job has been automated and we continue to delabor the sales process, making the sales org more efficient. Today, we're on the verge of the next evolution where the best products will actually sell themselves, and in order to stay relevant and compete, enterprise companies will need to adopt these product-led Sales Engagement strategies.

Leverage Your Product Data

Every lead is not created equal; neither is every customer. Successful sales teams understand that there are a common set of triggers that compel decision makers to move forward. Rather than looking for external triggers like a new hire, funding, or rapid growth, as we have done in the past, it's time to turn to your product. You can actually see what your users are doing—are they engaging with the product? Coming back for more? Sharing it with others in your company? Running into a friction point?

Figure out what the triggers are that indicate interest and will lead to a sale or expansion—maybe they need to invite another user, set up a schedule, create a timecard, or run their first report. When combined with demographic data, these product triggers will elevate the most important prospects for you to spend time with. Sales by no means goes away in a product-led growth model. Instead, sales takes on a higher-level role and engages with only the top-most prospects.

The key is to leverage your knowledge of your ICP (which now includes product data) to point your resources at the right free trial leads and existing customers ready for expansion.

Review Your Sales Process for Manual Processes

The sales tech stack is ever-expanding, and there are constantly new and creative ways to deleverage your sales process. It can seem daunting to make these changes, but the key is to build and iterate over time—this is not all or nothing. A few examples to try include:

- **Lead enrichment**: How much time does your sales team spend researching leads to determine basic demographic information used in qualification? Over time, we have watched companies take this responsibility away from Account Executives and move it to SDRs and then to Lead Specialists or even offshore teams. But there are many solutions that can help you remove hours per week of manual effort and automatically augment the lead data you capture on forms. Start testing solutions like Clearbit, ZoomInfo, and DataFox to see what works best for you. Still can't get the data you need?

- **Prospect engagement**: A tool that manages sequences is almost table stakes at this point. The key is in how these solutions are deployed—thoughtful messaging, A/B testing, minimal exceptions to the standard process, and constant iteration.

- **Appointment scheduling**: Put yourself in the customer's shoes. You want to get a few questions answered to determine whether you should be evaluating a product. You submit a form online and get a call from an SDR or sales rep. The best teams call you back right way, but many call you back hours and even days later and then use that time to try to book a future product demo. The lag time kills you. What if you could eliminate this back and forth and cut right to the end goal—a scheduled demo?

Align the Entire Team Around the Customer Experience

I don't want to point fingers, but it's oh so common in an organization to lay blame. Didn't hit your number this month? Missed a goal? The natural response is an excuse: "Well, the lead count from Marketing was down." This lack of alignment leads to an aggressive and often ill-informed approach to go-to-market and to communication with the customer. Conversion rate falling? Call the leads more. That's definitely what the decision maker who hasn't answered any of your 11 e-mails was hoping for.

I've done quite a bit of "mystery shopping" to see what happens when you submit a form or sign up for a new product. You'd be shocked at what I've found. It runs the gamut from never hearing back to 45 touches from seven different channels—SDR calls/e-mails, marketing e-mails from multiple systems, Intercom chats, texts from the product team—and no coordinated message or call to action.

Here's what you need to do: First, put the customer at the center of everything you do. Second, act like a team. Seriously, it's that simple. If customer experience is at the center of your decision making, you will naturally make different choices in your approach to channels. In practice, your goal should be to lead with product. If the customer falls out of your product funnel, use marketing to drive them back in, which allows you to focus on efficient many-to-one interactions. You can then apply human Sales Engagement to only the most important prospects and customers.

These are just three examples of how to apply a product-led approach to deleverage your sales process. The concept of automating away manual processes is not new—we've been doing it in software sales for more than 40 years, but it's accelerating quickly. As sales leaders, the only way to remain relevant is to adapt to the new trends and keep our teams focused on the interactions that really matter.

Liz is spot-on here. The future for sales is a bright one, with many innovations starting to flower as we speak. However, like anything else innovative, as soon as you hit the pinnacle, that's when you know it's time to refresh. Keep testing and thriving to get more efficient. Keep cycling channels. Keep looking for ways to get better. It's a constant process that never ends.

Summary

I n many ways, B2B selling has become a whole new world. Sellers—who for the most part of human history unilaterally defined the playing field—have found themselves far less relevant in the selling dynamic. Buyers will engage only with transparent, customer-focused advisors, and smooth-talking but snake-oil salespeople focused only on *their own* numbers will be instantly dismissed. After all, buyers already know quite a bit about your product. What they want to discover is whether they can trust the people behind it and whether the experience in buying and using your product will be worth their while. Ultimately, they need honest, personalized, relevant, and expert advice. Not another sales pitch.

The buyer's journey is more sophisticated than ever. The Internet not only empowered buyers with greater access to information and alternative solutions to their problems, but it also exponentially expanded the scope of omnichannel marketing. Omnichannel both deeply complicates the sale *and* offers an exciting opportunity to deliver the most customized and relevant buying experience in human history. Sales is truly at the edge of a sweeping new frontier, ripe for the taking.

Yet even in an ocean of change, you'll find constants that ground the new landscape. Respect, honesty, humanization, and creativity, for example, will remain relevant unless people cease being, well, human!

In the end, buyer centricity is both the old and new calculus and customer experience is both an emerging yet timeless currency. Today, tomorrow, and always, your value as a brand rises and falls on how much you value your buyers. Their time is precious. Gaining and keeping their attention is priceless.

In this book, we took you through how Sales Engagement solves seven of the most critical business pain points. The key takeaways include:

1. Make sure to optimize for how the modern buyer likes to buy. They're generational, always-on, and omnichannel. Sequences, personas, empathy, and humanization of sales content is key to modern Sales Engagement. To help understand your buyer, make sure your Sales, Marketing, and Customer Success teams are fully aligned.

2. Revenue Efficiency (doing more with less) with a growth-focused team can actually become a thing at your company! Not just a guess but knowing for sure what's driving revenue and being able to prove it to your boss, CEO, board, or shareholders will be a gamechanger. With modern Sales Engagement strategies, we can fully understand our pipeline and which levers to pull to increase our numbers.

3. Sales no longer needs to be so manual. With modern Sales Engagement that ties to account-based strategies, reps can get back to doing selling activities and *only* selling activities, which means they can get time back to do the things that move the needle.

4. You now have the know-how and ability to build consistent, repeatable, and data-driven processes, leveraging your understanding of executive-level metrics to track and how to track them. To take it a step further, with a Sales Engagement Platform, you will have access to data you would never normally have, and now you know how to get the most out of it!

5. Now we can improve new hire time to value. We know this is an area of pain for most sales leaders because every day a rep isn't fully

ramped is a day that the team is not at their full potential. However, with a modern Sales Engagement process rooted, we can ramp reps faster in a repeatable, replicable, and systematic manner.

6. We no longer lack the data necessary to drive business decisions. With the ability to A/B test our entire outreach process, we can fully understand the best actions to take across our entire revenue org.

7. Don't let tech stack troubles get you down. It's true that CRM, phone, and e-mail are no longer enough, but modern sales technology is easy to implement and easy to attribute ROI to.

There's still a lot to discover in the future of sales—labyrinths to navigate and new opportunities to exploit. But there are also a few givens that can help businesses set the right strategic directions. Certainly, B2B sales won't change course and retrace their way back to seller-centricity any time soon. If anything, the modern buying experience will move ever closer to the buyer, who already holds every key that matters. The sellers that accept and embrace this paradigm shift will win the arms race and emerge victorious in the most complicated selling playing field in human history.

We wrote this book because we care about our customers. When you win, we win. We're here to help you be among these proven winners in this new era of Sales Engagement.

Glossary

A/B Testing—A/B testing (also known as split testing or multivariable testing) is a method of comparing two or more variants against each other to determine which one performs better. A/B testing is essentially an experiment where two variants of a page are shown to users at random, and statistical analysis is used to determine which variation performs better for a given conversion goal.

Account Executive (AE)—Account Executives are the sales reps that are charged with moving the leads passed over from Sales Development Reps and closing the deals. They have a set revenue number they must hit each month in closed business, commonly known as "hitting quota."

Business to Business (B2B)—Business to business refers to commerce between two businesses rather than to commerce between a business and an individual consumer.

Customer Relationship Manager (CRM)—A Customer Relationship Manager is a system of record where reps manually log sales activities for management visibility.

CxO—CxO is a short way to refer, collectively, to corporate executives at what is sometimes called the C-level, whose job titles typically start with "Chief" and end with "Officer." CxO titles include Chief Executive

Officer (CEO), Chief Marketing Officer (CMO), Chief Information Officer (CIO), etc.

Data—A collection of empirically correct statistics and analysis for reference on a given topic.

Decision Maker (DM)—The decision maker in a sales funnel is the person who has buying authority and can make the official final decision to purchase a product or service.

General Data Protection Regulation (GDPR)—The General Data Protection Regulation is a legal framework that sets guidelines for the collection and processing of personal information of individuals within the European Union (EU). GDPR came into effect across the EU on May 25, 2018.

Ideal Customer Profile (ICP)—An ideal customer profile is a snapshot of desirable attributes and demographics that describe a company's ideal buyer—that is, company size, title, role, etc.

Marketing Qualified Lead (MQL)—A prospect or potential buyer that Marketing has evaluated and deemed worthy of passing over to Sales.

Omnichannel—Omnichannel is a cross-channel content strategy that organizations use to improve their user experience. Rather than working in parallel, communication channels and their supporting resources are designed and orchestrated to cooperate. Omnichannel implies integration and orchestration of channels such that the experience of engaging across all the channels someone chooses to use is as, or even more, efficient or pleasant than using single channels in isolation.

Personalization—Personalized marketing is the implementation of a strategy by which companies deliver individualized content to recipients through data collection, analysis, and the use of automation technology.

The goal of personalized marketing is to truly engage customers or prospective customers by communicating with each as an individual.

Personas—A buyer persona is a semifictional representation of the ideal customer based on market research and real data about existing customers. When creating buyer persona(s), consider including customer demographics, behavior patterns, motivations, and goals. The more detailed, the better.

Relevance—Relevance in sales communication is, in a nutshell, the opposite of spam. Rather, sales communications that have relevance are interesting and useful to the recipient and address an acute business problem or current and timely challenge for the prospect, thus creating active engagement between the seller and the buyer.

Sales Accepted Leads (SALs)—A lead that has been passed through from Marketing and accepted by Sales as a valid lead, aka someone who fits the accepted criteria of a buyer.

Sales Development Rep (SDR)—Also known as a Business Development Rep (BDR), a Sales Development Rep is a type of inside sales rep that solely focuses on outbound prospecting. Unlike quota-carrying salespeople, SDRs don't focus on closing business. Rather, SDRs focus on moving leads through the pipeline.

Sales Engagement Platforms (SEPs)—Sales Engagement Platforms enable reps to automate, analyze, and optimize their sales communications across all major sales channels to exponentially increase conversion.

Sequences—Sequences are a series of sales communications touchpoints triggered within a buyer's journey. Sequences are made of automated triggers to send the right message from the right medium at the right time. For example, a sequence may include a phone call, then a follow-up e-mail, and then a LinkedIn message, etc.

Service Level Agreement (SLA)—A Service Level Agreement is a contract between a service provider (either internal or external) and the end user that defines the level of service expected from the service provider. SLAs are output-based in that their purpose is specifically to define what the customer or recipient will receive. In this case, an agreement made internally between sales reps regarding the responsibilities of both parties when dealing with a new buyer or customer.

Acknowledgments

I t is fitting that we wrapped up writing this book the week of Thanksgiving here in the United States. It is with great gratitude that we thank our wonderful customers, our community, and our own Outreachers who contributed to this book. The coolest part about writing this book was writing it with all of you.

A big Outreach-style thank you to our customers and partners and those helping us shape the new landscape of modern sales, allowing salespeople to do more than ever before—and do it better—with Sales Engagement. These modern sellers and sales leaders are producing better results, with more efficiency, and are creating a better buying experience for customers all over.

This book would not have been possible without the wisdom and expertise of so many, including (in alphabetical order):

Lauren Alt, Marketing Campaigns Manager at Outreach

Brooke Bachesta, Sales Development Manager at Outreach

Lauren Bailey, CEO of Factor 8

Scott Barker, Head of Partnerships at Sales Hacker

John Barrows, CEO of JBarrows Training

Ralph Barsi, Senior Director of Global Sales Development at ServiceNow

Tito Bohrt, CEO of AltiSales

Jennifer Brandenburg, Vice President of Worldwide Inside Sales at GE Digital

Elizabeth Cain, Partner at OpenView Venture Partners

Jessica Cross, Manager, Demand Generation, at a prominent high-growth AdTech company

Pavel Dmitriev, Vice President of Data Science at Outreach

Jake Dunlap, CEO of Skaled

Chad Dyar, Director of Sales Enablement at OnDeck

Todd Eby, Co-founder of SuccessHACKER

Mario Espinoza, Operations Manager at Outreach

Dan Gottlieb, Sales Development Industry Analyst at TOPO Inc.

Alex Greer, CEO of Signal HQ

Richard Harris, CEO of The Harris Consulting Group

Rob Jeppsen, CEO of Xvoyant

Jonathan A. Mayer, Senior Manager of Business Development at Splunk

Sam Nelson, Sales Development Manager at Outreach

David Priemer, Chief Sales Scientist at Cerebral Selling

Ben Salzman and Kyle Williams, Co-founders of Dogpatch Advisors

Amy Slater, Vice President of Corporate Sales of Palo Alto Networks

Jen Spencer, Vice President of Sales and Marketing at SmartBug Media

Julianne Thompson, Sales Development Manager at Outreach

Jason Vargas, Co-founder and Evangelist of CopyShoppe.co

Last but not least, a massive thank you to our team of incredibly talented, hardworking, and genuinely great people at Outreach. And an extra special thank you to those Outreachers who worked on the book directly, including Jade Makana, Director of Content at Outreach; Maggie Anthoney, Senior Legal Counsel at Outreach; Joan Mirano, our Lead Virtual Assistant; and many others.

Bonus Content!

Visit SalesEngagement.com for more educational resources on all things Sales Engagement.

Visit us at Outreach.io to learn more about the leading Sales Engagement platform.

About the Authors

Manny **Medina** co-founded Outreach, the industry's leading sales engagement software, in 2014 and now serves as CEO. Prior to Outreach, Manny was employee number three on Amazon's AWS team and led the Microsoft mobile division from launch to $50 M in annual revenue. He holds an MBA from Harvard and a master's in computer science from the University of Pennsylvania. Manny is a model of vulnerable and transparent leadership to his employees, from his heartfelt weekly email, "From the CEO's desk," to the traditional Friday get-together, Boot, where the whole company shares their shout-outs and highs and lows of the week. He championed a groundbreaking maternity/paternity plan and is a proponent of saving the planet by consuming less and purchasing secondhand whenever possible (he might be the only CEO to take the stage at industry events in shirts purchased from Goodwill). Manny grew up in Ecuador and now lives with his wife and three children in Seattle.

Max Altschuler is the Vice President of Marketing at Outreach and the CEO of Sales Hacker. He started Sales Hacker in 2013 and built it up to a more than 100,000-member community for B2B sales professionals. In 2018, Sales Hacker was acquired by Outreach, and Max became the VP of Marketing. An early convert of the Sales Engagement movement, Max became involved with Outreach in the early days as an investor, then as a customer, and then as an executive in 2018. He is an avid early stage startup investor and advisor to more than 55 companies. When he's not maniacally focused on helping sales orgs exponentially increase their results with Sales Engagement, he spends time with his partner, Ashley, and two King Charles Cavaliers, Brie and Tini. He also donates his time and energy to helping women and military veterans build careers in tech and to animal rescues, including Muttville Senior Dog Rescue.

Mark Kosoglow was the first employee of Outreach and now serves as the Vice President of Sales. He earned his bachelor's in marketing at Pennsylvania State University and after 25 years in sales and sales management, Mark came to a conclusion: Sales is broken. Too many sales people fail, and too many managers can't help. Luckily, a series of events led to a meeting with Manny Medina, which allowed Mark to see that not only was it possible to fix sales but also that he could be a part of the solution. So Mark joined Outreach in 2014 as its first "employee" (he took the job as a 100% commissioned contractor) with a personal mission of helping more sales professionals win. Mark recently moved to Seattle with his wife, Julie; daughters, Maqqel and Mia; and sons, Sam and Emmanuel (Eman), where they enjoy doing things together like hosting Thanksgiving dinners for all the other Outreach Seattle transplants who stay in the area for the holidays.

Index